GREAT MINDS ARE GREAT ACHIEVERS

Lawrence Ativie Osifo

LAWRENCE *Ativie* **OSIFO**

For spiritual counseling and helps write or come to:

Lawrence Ativie Osifo
Coordinator – Leaders Forum International
23A; Isibor Street;
Off Stadium Road; Benin City
+234-8027892423; +234-8094748162; +234-8068045329
aghatemwosa@gmail.com

CONTENTS

INTRODUCTION
GREATNESS MINDSET

Great minds are great achievers. Generation now and the next should be strongly imparted and inspired with this idea by everyone who has the authority to influence them.

It is the duty of every teacher to transfer such knowledge into every student taught by them. Every leader is a teacher and for any leader to end up successfully; he or she must have a great mindset or idea which has been taught or passed on to a successor. Therefore; I have this idea that "Great minds are great Achievers" to teach or to impart into the mindset of this and coming generation. It will be a laudable and an effective solution to the present world unrest if every parent; every political leader; every religious leader and every academic leader; would counsel, proclaim, preach and teach this idea; that "Great Minds are Great Achievers"; to their children, their constituencies; their congregations and their schools.

If fifty percent of the people living on earth are able to have this mindset that; "Great Minds are Great Achievers"; the victory over evil will be easily achieved without the use of weapons of war. Imparting this idea into the conscience of mankind stands out as the greatest legacy we can bequeath to the next generation as well as the best service we can give to God.

The amazing phenomenon of this wonderful idea; of "Great Minds are Great Achievers"; is that those who have great mindset are ever willing to impart the inspiration into others.

As a Civil Engineering graduate; but employed to teach mathematics in secondary school; I tried to be practical in my teaching method so that my students would understand and become great and outstanding persons in the future. Therefore, I was always giving or citing instances and issues of life where mathematics could be practically applied. It was in the process I got the idea to write this book.

Great mindset has undergone a kind of evolution from the mean state of human lifestyle to a higher state of mental freedom for effective living. Great minds are like very sensitive antenna of radio receiver. Great minds have highly sensitive perception of the spiritual information. Great minds are able to catch revelations from the realm of the spirits to create wealth and to live freely from fears and anxieties.

Great minds have the **Christ-like** *hearts that think only of greatness or of things beyond the earth realm.*

They are minds that dwell in Great ideas. I believe that you would want to be in greatness. The 'How to have a Great mind'; has **Desire** as the ultimate step; whether it is taken first or lastly. *This desire can be called FAITH.*

The makeup of great desires includes ambitious attitude, bold beliefs, contented commitment, disciplined diligence, and dutiful determination.

There are three steps into greatness; that could be called three categories of greatness.

1.   Born into greatness
2.   Bestowed with greatness
3.   Believed or achieved greatness.

The third step which is believed or achieved greatness; I wish to classify this stage as the ultimate; most rewarding and peaceful. One is only graduated to this level by his earnest desire.

A preacher somewhere; after speaking on the benefits of praises to God; put forth this question: *"Can anyone; in this place; who had contributed in any way to his or her being alive today put up his hand?"* I was the only person who put up his hand.

As I did; I looked foolish to every other person in that meeting. It is always like that when a man; by faith; turns to Christ. He will look foolish; carnally considering his decision. His friends and neighbours will begin to mock at him. So; I was foolish to these people who did not fully understand the preacher's question. Then he asked me; *"My friend, how have you contributed to your being alive today?"*

"I have given my life to God. I am now born of the Spirit and I submitted myself for water baptism. There I was buried with Christ and resurrected with Him; and He now lives my life for me. As I gave my life to Him He **adopted** *me. Now I* **believe** *I am great and* **alive** *in Christ; as my Lord".*

Someone without a desire or ambition; no matter the bequeathed wealth; or even a royal birth, he or she cannot attain unto greatness. *You should earnestly desire to be living in greatness.* Just earnestly

"**Desire**" to be a great achiever; and you will become one of the world's famous celebrities.

Life in greatness is all that a man requires; tobe ever healthy, attractive to favors, enjoying peace and prosperity, be a winner all the time, promoted promptly; be beyond destructions; beloved; above reproaches; and be freed fromcondemnations and oppressions.

CHAPTER ONE
GREATNESS

Greatness is an exalted position; an attractive estate; and a domain of fame, peace, respects, honor, favor, joy and successful opportunities. It is a situation and circumstance where one is no longer denied access to any place or anything good.

Greatness is freedom from molestation, condemnation, and lacks. It is a lifestyle apart from poverty, rejection, humiliation, and oppression.

In the position of Greatness no one sees your faults anymore.

We are in a world of *"rise up if you can or remain crawling if cannot rise "*. – quote Lawrence Ativie Osifo

In this world therefore; some persons are born great; some have greatness bestowed on them while others who are great, achieved greatness by their sincere desires.

The above citation defines the three steps into greatness – *Born into greatness, Adopted into greatness, and Achieved greatness.*

THE QUESTION: "HOW"

"How do people achieve greatness?"

People, who achieve greatness, *ask for it*, believe in it and claim it. Those who asked for and received greatness, usually have joyful, lasting, peaceful, enviable, dignified and fulfilled greatness.

"How do people **inherit** *greatness?"*

People, who inherit *greatness,* are adopted into wealth and thrones; - they *have greatness bestowed on them by their parents or masters.*

"How are people born into greatness?"

People, who are offspring of kings and great men, *are born great.* Some who are born great or are bestowed with greatness; do not actually have precious and enviable greatness. They sometimes become careless because they did not really go through the refining fire into greatness. The refining fire is the human trials of life to test the individual endurance ability.

As a living man you can be as great as you so desire if you are determined, diligent and disciplined. Your position in life depends on what you have ignorantly or knowingly chosen to be. Any man who is inferior and despised was not originally destined to be so. If we have to turn the page to look at it on the both sides, we will always arrive at the same answer that *God, the creator, is impartialbecause in His wisdom made every man to live in Greatness*

Some people who were *born little* have had the opportunity to achieve greatness. These ones were not born by kings or lords. They were bequeathed properties by rich parents. They used their opportunities (as long as they had life) to struggle, strived or climbed into greatness. Example was *Jabez;* in the bible book of *1Chronicles 4:10. And Jabez made a prayer to the God of Israel, saying, If only you would truly give me a blessing, and make wider the limits of my land, and let your hand be with me, and keep me from evil, so that I may not be troubled by it! And God gave him his desire.*

No man therefore has any excuse whatsoever to remain mean and wanting. Believe that you can be great; that you can be productive, that you can succeed, that you can prosper, etc. As long as God does not restrict the breath of life to anyone, as long as God does not physically kill any man, (evil slays the wicked) every man has the same privilege to live and to achieve greatness; for righteousness is what exalts a person. *You are great when you are a child of a great man. You are great when a great man adopts you to inherit his properties. You are great when you make yourself to walk on the path of greatness.*

The First step is that you are born great. The Second is that greatness is bestowed on you, and the third, is that you achieved greatness by your desires and deeds.

THE WISDOM OF GOD

In the wisdom of God; the pathway to greatness is narrow. You must be spiritually born and adopted into the system. You have to thereafter be determined to abide in that position by your desire, wisdom, and faith in the person who has begotten or adopted you.

You have to **believe his word, receive his spirit, and keep his commandments.**

The wisdom of God always appear mysterious and unwise to the unlearned and the unconverted.

The holy bible book of *Galatians 2:20; says; I am crucified with Christ: nevertheless I live; yet not I, but Christ lives in me: and the life which I now live in flesh I live by the faith of the son of God who loved, and gave Himself for me.*

"Now I believe I shall inherit the kingdom of God with Christ". *I shall not die but live to declare the work of God; says the book of Psalms 118:17.*

I am born into greatness.

I am bestowed with greatness.

I believe or I can achieve greatness.

When one is born again, the Lord adopts him, and he becomes a great personality. In other words, whoever receives Jesus as Lord is born into Greatness.

YOU MUST BE BORN GREAT:

Nicodemus came to Jesus the Christ by night, with the intention to know how to be a reputable individual. He began to enumerate the observable and enviable qualities of greatness in Jesus Christ. *In the bible book of John 3:2; he said unto Him, "Rabbi, we know that you are a teacher from God: for no man can do these miracles that you do, except God be with him.* He desired to be renowned as well, but did not know exactly how to go about it. *Jesus answered and said to him, most assuredly I say to you, unless one is born again (born great) he cannot see the kingdom of God (Step into greatness).* Nicodemus did not understand but Christ went further to explain that it was not the physical rebirth but a spiritual transformation of the heart that can translate any man into the realm of greatness. – The kingdom of the children of God. - *Those that were not born of blood or of the will of the flesh nor of the will of man but of God; as recorded in John 1:13.*

One must be regenerated in thoughts and outlook to the things of life before elevation into greatness.

Stepping into greatness is by faith.

The great aspirant must begin to see his desires as possible with God. He sees God as the great provider who cannot lie nor deceive any one. He puts off the natural Adam's ways or manner of reasoning and acting.

The bible book of 2Corinthians 5:17; says; If any man be in Christ, he is a new creation, old things (old method of planning, and execution of projects) are passed away, behold all things have become new (new approaches to lifestyle etc). John 1:12; says; as many as received Him (Christ as their Lord and personal savior) to them gave Him the right to become the children of God, to those who believe in His name; (Those who believe that the store house of God is full of great things).

When you have been born great, then your great father will begin to bequeath his wealth to you. He has to adopt you into His position or else you remain a slave. A slave is ruled by fear. A son freely lives with the father and enjoys all rights.

YOU MUST BE ADOPTED

When one has been born great, then he begins to exhibit faith in his great father. The faith is that he believes and wants to be like him. Until one has had enough courage to believe in this great father, He will not permit him or her to inherit his properties. *But when the fullness of the time had come, God sent forth His son, to redeem those who were under the law (those without faith to be great) that we might receive the adoption as sons. And because you are sons, God has sent forth the Spirit of His Son into your hearts, crying out Abba, Father! Therefore you are no slave but a son; an heir of God through Christ. - (Galatians 4:4-7). For as many as are led by the Spirit of God, they are the sons of God. The Spirit itself bears witness with our spirit, that we are the children of God (Romans 8:14, 16).*

You are only worthy of the bounties of God when you are His child. You are His child when you have His Spirit in you. You have His Spirit inside of you when He adopts you. *Your adoption is complete, when you believe in His Word and in the power of the Holy Spirit.*

The Spirit of the Holy God is the Spirit of power - the Spirit that believes that all things are possible. - The Spirit that is pure and holy and the Spirit that is determined, diligent and disciplined. - The spirit that does not faint in times of trials and temptations. – The spirit that is not deceitful but truthful, sincere and honest. - The spirit that not fearful but bold. That is the Spirit of greatness - *the Spirit of faith that is able to take giant strides; is a great mind.*

Your Consent Is Required; When you are to be adopted by any person you have to agree or disagree as the case may be. Your agreement must be communicated either verbally or by conduct. If you agree, then you are expected to obey the will of your foster parent.

The bible book of Romans 6:16; asks; do you not Know that to whoever you yield yourselves as servants to obey, His servants you are; - to whom you obey whether of sin unto death, or of obedience unto righteousness?

Note that whosoever adopts you requires your absolute obedience and co-operations. It is not the character of the great person to be faithless, stubborn or rebellious.

But when you are stubborn; and you are rebellious and wicked to your benefactor; then you lack faith in him. He will not permit you to inherit him. This was the case against Saul the first king in Israel.

And Samuel said, has the Lord as great delight in burnt offerings and sacrifices, as in obeying the voice of the Lord? Behold, to obey is better than sacrifice, and to hearken than the fat of rams. - For rebellion is as the sin of witchcraft, and stubbornness is as iniquity and idolatry. Because thou have rejected the word of the Lord, He has also rejected thee from being king. (1 Samuel 15:22-23).

You Have To Change Your Name; this is real faith in action. You must change your name as a sign or a token of covenant. Your name is your identity. This is likened to marriage. When a woman is married to **Evangelist**, Ativie Lawrence Osifo she must begin to bear the name; Mrs. Osifo hence forth, or else, she is not yet consented to the marriage. An adopted child must of necessity change his or her name to the name of the foster father.

Your change of name has much to do with knowing who you are. God changed the name of Abram to Abraham to make him know that he was a father of nations. The book of *Genesis 17:4-5; says as for Me, (God speaking) behold, My covenant is with you, and you shall be a father of many nations. Neither shall thy name be any more called Abram, but thy name shall be Abraham; for a father of many nations have I made you.* Jacob was changed to Israel.

In Genesis 32:38; God said, your name shall be called no more Jacob, but Israel: for as a prince you have power with God and with men, and has prevailed;

My name also is changed spiritually, from failure to success. - *Jesus is my Lord. My name is:* **Lawrence, Precious Throne.** You can change your own name also. Not necessarily physically but spiritually. *In John 1:12; the scripture; says; as many as received him, to them He gave power to become the sons of God, even those that believe on His name;*

The book of Romans 8:17; says; if children, then heirs; heirs of God, and joint-heirs with Christ; if so be that we suffer withHim, that we may also be glorified together.

Moses refused to be called an Egyptian when he discovered that he was a Jew. Jabez; also changed his own name from *pain to progress.* Jabez's name was given to him by his mother to mean pain. He grew up to be a sorrowful person. Circumstances and situations were always working against him. He was often disappointed, frustrated and despised. But when he realized that he must be great to have the yoke broken, then he ASKED for a change of name by submitting himself to the God of Israel; in 1Chronicles 4:9-10. *He asked for a change from **grief** to **great.***When you submit to God, and preach or teach His word great will be your rewards on earth and in heaven.

*Daniel 12:3; says; they that will be wise (**great minds**) shall shine as brightness of the firmament and they that turn many to righteousness as the stars forever and ever.*

YOU MUST HAVE A STRONG DESIRE FOR GREATNESS. It is one thing to be born great and be adopted by a great man. It is another thing altogether to achieve greatness. When one does not have the *mind* to be great, even though he is born by a king, and thousands of thousands of gifts are bestowed on him he will still remain mean or miserable.

An African adage in Edo language, titled:

"Ule-le-fe-nogha-rhue-ru"; says, that the fortune seeker that desires to be crowned will be crowned though an elephant should tread on it many times grinding it to pieces. *One that is marked for greatness, however the frustrations, if he desires to be, he will surely be when he or she works towards it.* Even if there is no mark of greatness on anyone, when he begins to desire or pray for greatness, the spirit of greatness will come upon him.

It is *The Spirit of greatness that is the great mindset that attracts greatness.*

When anyone desires to work miracles like Christ, His Spirit will come upon him and he will become a great and miraculous person also. *Verily, verily, I say unto you, he that believes on Me, (Jesus Christ speaking) the works that I do shall he do also; and greater works than these shall he do; because I go unto My Father; in John 14:12.*

Now, whosoever sees him will accordingly notice the star of greatness on him. What I am saying is that, you should not be deceived to believe that greatness is for some specially elected individuals in life. No! But for those who desire or have *great minds*; to be and are determined to be. "You can be great if you desire and work for it". In *1Chronicles 4:10; And Jabez called unto the God of Israel saying "Oh that you would bless me indeed, and enlarge my territory, that your hand would be with me, and that I may not cause pain" So God granted him what he requested.*

Jabez was like any other person living on earth today. *But the God he believed in made the difference.*

Hebrews 13:8; say that Jesus Christ is the same yesterday and today, and into the ages to come. The God of Israel has not changed. He does not and He will not change. But He can change our situations and circumstances when we pray Him to, and when we change our attitude.

YOU MUST PRAY

The realization of greatness by any person requires more than the ordinary human efforts. The crown of greatness is usually settled in the spiritual realm before the physical manifestation. Although, the crowning is the Lord's doing, the efforts of man are still very much essential. If Joseph had not been diligent enough to effectively and undauntedly follow the leading of God, he would have not been crowned. *In Genesis 41:38-39; Pharaoh said unto his servants could we find such a one, as this is, a man in whom the Spirit of God is? And pharaoh said unto Joseph, for as much as God has showed you all these, there is none as discreet and wise as you art.*

If God does not find a righteous man with a "DESIRE" at any point in time, He usually apply His sovereignty to elect a "permitted" person or someone who has determination to succeed or one with a *Great Mind* or one who **prays at all**. *Isaiah 59:16 says; He saw that there was no man, and wondered that there was no intercessor:*

therefore His own arm brought salvation unto Him; and His righteousness it sustained Him.

The element of agreement is that there must be a **prayer** or "Desire and willingness" by the recipient for an adoption to stand.

Someone must be having great thoughts to agree with the spirit for two persons cannot walk together except that they agree.

The agreement from man is communicated to God by his *'prayers and offerings'* and the confirmation from God is by fire. *Now when Solomon had made an end of praying, the fire came down from heaven, and consumed the burnt offering and the sacrifices; and the glory of the LORD filled the house. Then the king and all the people offered sacrifices before the LORD. And the LORD appeared to Solomon by night, and said to him, I have heard your prayer and have chosen this place to myself for a house of sacrifice.*

God is earnestly waiting for you to sincerely desire and to claim your promotion in life. He says; in the book of Matthew 11:28-30 *"Come unto Me, all of you that have labored and are heavily laden, and I will give you rest. Take my yoke upon you, and learn from me for I am meek and lowly in heart: and you shall find rest for your souls. My yoke is easy and My burden is light".*

Prayer is an expression of the heart's desire. It is the means of communication with the source of supply of the required greatness. Prayer is ASKing. That is to: Ask, Seek, and Knock or (ASK). Any one, who must successfully enter into greatness, must go beyond the mere "Wishing" to "persistent ASKing". To *ask* is to make a verbal request of that which is greatly and tirelessly desired.

To *seek* is to go beyond asking to knock. Everyone is advised to cease to pursue the doctrine of pre-destination as an excuse for indolence. Just back up your strong desires with determinations and *fervent prayers and hard working* then you will be into greatness. *Do you see a man diligent in his business? He shall stand before kings; he shall not stand before mean men.*

To knock is to increase the tempo or intensity of a desire by taking actions. *Everyone who asks receives, and he who seeks finds, and to him who knocks it will be opened.* Jacob was well aware of these principles; *will, work and watch*; and he never failed to practice them.

In the book of *Genesis 32:24, 26; Jacob; wrestling with angel; the angel said, "Let me go, for the day breaks" but he said, "I will not let you go unless you bless me".*

Prayer can also be a kind of wrestling with God. *In Luke 18:1;* Christ says: *Men ought always to pray and not to faint (not to be discourage, tired, etc)* The courage and the tirelessness are as a result of being born great; then one becomes possessed by the Spirit of the great God (Another spirit).

CHAPTER TWO
ANOTHER SPIRIT

But my servant Caleb because he has a different (another) spirit in him and has followed (have faith in) me fully, I will bring into the land where he went and his descendants shall inherit it (he shall be great) (Numbers 14:24). The spirit that is undaunted, determined, resolute, diligent, disciplined, desperate, persistent, and faithful. - *The spirit that thinks greatly and sees possibilities.* This different spirit was the kind of spirit in the Heroes of faith.

"Abraham":

*For what does the scripture say? Abraham **believed** God, and it was accounted to him for righteousness (Romans 4:30).*

"Moses":

*By faith Moses, when he became of age, **refused** to be called the son of pharaoh's daughter... **choosing** the people of God... **esteeming** Christ greater riches, looked to the reward by faith; **forsook** Egypt... he **endured**.... as **seeing** him who is invisible. - (Hebrews 11:24-28).*

"Daniel":

The book of Daniel 1:8; says; *But Daniel **purposed** in his heart that he would **not defile** himself with the portion of the king's delicacies, or with the wine, which he drank. Therefore he **requested** of the chief of the eunuchs that he might not defile himself.*

"Esther":

In the book of Esther 4: 15-25; *Then Esther **told** them to reply to Mordecai to gather all the Jews who were present in Shushan, 'and **fast** for me; neither eat nor drink for three days, night or day. My maids and I will fast likewise. And so I will go to the king (great people dine with the king), which is against the law, **and if I perish, I perish.'***

"Joseph":

*In Genesis 39:9, 12; **Joseph** said, there is no one greater in this house than I, nor has he kept back anything from mebut you, because you are his wife. **How then can I do** this great wickedness, and sin against God? **He left his garment in her hand,** and **fled and ran** outside.*

Notice that in all these personalities above, none of them agreed to settle for any temporary or lesser positions. *They all possessed great minds that could see the brighter future.* This **"Another spirit"** is different from the kind in mean men or the **spirit of fear**. 2*Timothy 1:7; says; God has not given us the spirit of fear; but of power, and of love, and of a sound mind.*

POSSESS A GREAT MIND

If you want to be great, famous and be one of the celebrities, you must possess a **great mind. Little minds** are timid and narrow in their thoughts or shortsighted in vision. They discuss people, gossip, murmur, and complain. They have Thomas' mind, which doubts and fear or always seeing impossibilities.

Average minds discuss events, and walk by sight. They only see those who have failed in so and so ventures. They walk by history and forecast. They lack enough faith to trust in God.

In the book of 2kings 7:2; then a lord on whose hand the king leaned answered the man of God, and said, behold, if the Lord would make windows in heaven, might this thing be? And he said, Behold, you shall see it with your own eyes, but shall not eat thereof.

Great minds discuss ideas. They are spiritually minded. They see God in action. They believe the impossible to be possible. They have great visions: In *2kings 7:1,18; the scripture says; then Elisha said, hear the word of the LORD; Tomorrow about this time shall a measure of fine flour be sold for a shekel, and two measures of barely for a shekel, in the gate of Samaria... And it came to pass as the man of God had spoken to the king, two measures of barely for a shekel, and a measure of fine flour for a shekel, were sold in the gate of Samaria.*

Great minds have miracle mindsets. They see beyond the ordinary or the physical. ***They put their faith in action.***

BELIEVE AND LIVE GREAT

There was a king who once traveled with his servant. On their way, the servant earnestly begged the master. "Please my master, do not call me a slave when we arrive at our destination". The master agreed but replied, *"I shall not call you a slave, but you; that is your own character; may personally call yourself a slave"*. Unfortunately for the slave, it rained heavily on them on the way and their clothes were soaked with water. When they arrived at their lodging, the king was bold enough to approach the master of the house for a change of apparel. But the servant took his raiment to the kitchen, and spread them on the place where meats are kept for seasoning, and squatted by the fire; to be warmed. When the steward of the lodging home saw these clothes on the kitchen drier, he exclaimed; *"who is this slave, that is so foolish, unlearned and careless to place his clothes here?"* His conduct betrayed him. Greatness or decency; was not in his character. Your action, attitude, and conduct or your character can tell others about you. *Actions speak louder than voices.* You can become great by imitating great characters like: love, kindness, righteousness, patience, and sincerity. You can become great by being peaceful, by being contented, not greedy, not slothful or timid but hardworking, diligent, determined and disciplined. *Great men do not argue blindly.They do not gamble through life.* Therefore, they do not begin to say, "I want to be like so and so man", just like that – without serious considerations of how to actualize their dreams. What godly qualities do you observe in that great man you desire to be like? Simply pray to God; saying, *'Oh LORD, work these characters in me'.* Otherwise, you can pray; *"LORD; use me according to Your will. I desire to do exploit for You'. Make me great. Make me to excel in my endeavors".* Then, in your works, begin to pray against all odds; hindrances and obstacles that may want to disallow your progress. Observe the behavior of worthless men, and avoid them. For example; the bible says that you should not walk with an angry man or you will learn his ways. Also whosoever is angry with his brother shall be guilty of hell fire; or such a miserable death.

Anger and timidity are weak natures, which we should not emulate. You should not pray to be like the *anger filled* fellow. *You should not be fearful but bold; you should not be selfish but generous.* There are many so-called men of God who still have not mastered themselves. They still get angry uncontrollable, tell lies and cheat others; such cannot be grouped among great men. Some of them quote scriptures to support themselves that Christ got angry. If you desire greatness then you must despise anger. But for God's mercy Moses' anger would have killed him.

Great men are temperate and moderate in their ways. They are not gluttonous, neither are they covetous in conducts and desires. They do not get easily offended. Anger is not their virtue. Lust and greed also are not great virtues. Many Israelites lusted and they fell in the time of Moses.

Honor is given only to those who are sincerely, truly and righteously great. You know them by their fruit; they act lovingly, kindly, gentle, meekly, humbly, sincerely, and are faithful to promises; peaceful, not arrogant and not bossy.

Learn from them, only the godly virtues. Do not be a sycophant or praise singer to them or to any man. *If you do, you will be corrupted by flatteries.* **The bible book of** Daniel 11:32; says;*such as do wickedly against the covenant shall he corrupt by flatteries: but the people that do know their God shall be strong, and do exploits.*

Sycophants are ever subject to great men, and they hardly become great themselves.

If you are the type who respects, serves or follows people because of their flashy car and money, God is against you for despising the poor. *Humble yourself before God and He will exalt you in due time.*

BE ENCOURAGED

God was proud of Job's righteousness. *Job 1:8; says; the LORD said unto Satan, have you considered my servant Job, that there are none like him in the earth, a perfect and an upright man, one that feared God and eschewed evil?* When a child does a good thing his good father usually encourages him with precious gift.

God always employ this method to His children. A child who is thus treated is inspired to do more. And gradually the child will grow up with the character or habit of doing great things. Often you hear men and women in the society, making remarks concerning individuals of either good or bad conduct. Let your actions be always right. You can conveniently walk into greatness when you know the mind of God, and submit to His will. David was beloved in the sight of God because he was a man after God's own heart. He possessed a repentant heart. You can know more of the mind of God when you know much of the word of God. *1Peter 2:2; says; as newborn babies, desire the pure milk of the word that you may grow thereby. And 2Timothy 2:15; says; study to show your-self approved, a workman that needed not to be ashamed.*

The more you know the word of God, the more you get familiar with the great God who has begotten you and bequeathed His wealth to you. *In the book of John 5:39*; Jesus says; search *the scriptures; for in them you think you have eternal life; the scriptures testify of Me.*

The scriptures testify of Christ as the only source of greatness; as in John 14:6. He is also the *author of love as in John 3:16.*

Great minds practice true love towards all. Love enables you to forgive your offenders and pray for others. Love makes you able to accommodate others, no matter their status and conditions.

If you have no love as your character; you are not great. Without love you cannot be useful to God. Great men are useful men to God. Love makes a man bold, kind, and unselfish. When you are partial, as a leader, people will be scared off you. Greatness is not selfish and not partial.

Join the majority. One with God is majority. You can be in the majority when you possess Caleb's and Daniel's another spirit, by becoming the child of the great God. Invest your talents. Study extra more, and work harder than your counterparts in your field of endeavor.

TAKE GREAT RISK

When you have been born great, you must be prepared to take great risk to become a great person.

Associate yourself with great minded men and begin to fellowship in a church with the sound doctrine and with the love of God.

But be very careful; not all big places of fellowships practice true love. All that glitter is not gold.

Moses forsook the Egyptians palace to be with the people of the great God and King.

The Israelites crossed the red sea to get out of slavery.

Imagine, waters on both sides, and a sane people courageously step in between. There can be no greater risk than this.

The three Hebrew children – Shadrach, Meshech, and Abednego, saw the fiery furnace of Nebuchadnezzar; they still said; *"Oh king, we are not careful to answer you in this matter; Our God (Father) is able to deliver us out of the fire."*

Indeed God did deliver them. For He says, *when you pass through the waters, it will not overflow you;* like in the case of the Israelites crossing from Egypt to the other side. *If you go through the fire it will not kindle you;* like in the case of the three Hebrew children. What greater risk can be more than these or what greater risk can be more than Daniel's Den of lions? The great risks I want you to take include: *Throwing off all your idols and burning up all your occult books*.

I personally did it when I heard the message from a house fellowship. I took all the *Amok or Rosicrucian* monographs and the membership card to the corner of my house. As I sang; *"There is power in the blood; I am cover with the blood of Jesus"*, I made a burn fire of it all.

Another great risk is that you have to begin to tell your friends that the Great God has adopted you. If you have wronged any of them in the past, confess, and apologize to them and return all the stolen properties with you to the owners. I did this also as I prayerfully went to my father to confess my past disobedience and misdeed to him.

Importunate fasting prayers like of Christ and Moses, for forty days and forty nights, are also necessary risks that could be taken towards greatness.

When you have taken these great risks, then you have fulfilled the part of the scriptures that would bring the mighty blessings of God to you.

You have pleased God by your faith. *Hebrews 10:38; says; now they that are just shall live by faith: but if any man draws back, my soul shall have no pleasure in him*.

You have come to Him, and you have believed that He is able to promote you exceedingly. *For without faith it is impossible to please Him. For he that comes to God must believe that He is and that He rewards them that diligently seek Him; says Hebrews 11:6*. He will not now delay, but hasten to perform His promises towards you. *Jeremiah 1:12;* says *then said the LORD unto me, you have well seen: for I will hasten my word to perform it*. The promises of God include: *I will make you a great nation; I will bless you. And make your name great; and you shall be a blessing, I will bless those who bless you, and I will curse those who curse you: And in you all the families of the earth shall be blessed; says the bible book of Genesis 12:2*. Begin to appropriate these good promises and others in the Bible to yourself.

WALK CIRCUMSPECTLY

Fools rush in where angels fear to tread. Remember that I have told you earlier on that you have to know the mind of God concerning you and what you want to do, as a prerequisite for exaltation into His greatness.

There are times that one ignorantly and carnally makes wrong moves and then ends up at a blind alley. If your desired greatness is to travel out of your present location; perhaps to a place of greener pasture, I counsel you to primarily pray for the will of God concerning your destination.

When you refused to pray, you may arrive to your destination successfully, but, being that you have acted on the permissive will of God, things will be hard for you.

This is the reason; you find some people being duped or killed, repatriated or are not able to come back home profitably.

Some, when they return, do fall into the hands of devourers, witches and evil forces. If your desired greatness is a life partner, you must pray for the proper and perfect will of God. If children, you must not add cult to Christ. If for money, you must not cheat others for it.

As for those who pray for unrighteous fortune seekers, there is the need to exercise cautions so that the one you are pulling up does not drag you down into hell. We must be discreet and patient for God's will.

Granted that it is the will of God for His children to prosper; but God did not allow the Israelites to remain in Egypt for the sake of prosperity. *God did not encourage Israelites to go to Babylon.*

As a man of God, your duty is to direct the blind out of darkness into light. Do not compromise your faith. Do not begin to pray for every Tom, Dick and Harry for the sake of dollars they are willing to pay into your account.

Be sincere enough to tell them the mind of God on this issue of greatness and ambition. *1Timothy 5:22;* says; Lay *hands suddenly on no man, and do not be a partaker of other men's sins: keep yourself pure.* Remember what Christ says, *not all that said Lord, Lord shall inherit God's kingdom.* Please, be wise like serpent but harmless like the DOVE.

BE STRONG

The bible book of Joshua 1:7; says; "Only be strong and very courageous, that you may observe to do according to all the law which Moses my servant commanded you; do not turn from it to the right hand or to the left hand, that you may prosper wherever you go".Prosperity is greatness.

The laudable and godly methods to prosperity stand out as *'diligence and determination'*.

"Ule-le-fe" or the fortune seeker is an ant mould; (not ant hill); usually found in the tropical forest. It says that, though an elephant should tread on it several times, it will be capped, if it desires to be capped. This little ant mould usually found in the tropical rain forest, is often about 30cm high, barrel-like in shape and about 10cm in diameter. This little termite structure is called *Ule-le-fe* in Edo language. Most of the times, this little mould is with a conical cap.

The Binis have a proverb made by personifying this ant mould, saying, *"The Ule-le-fe that will be capped will surely be capped, even if an elephant should tread on it and ground it to powder several times"*. The above proverb teaches *all* that the "big ones" (those who have made it) - just cannot prevent the *'little ones'* from wearing crowns if they (who have not made it) are so determined. There is a saying that "if you cannot beat them, you have to join them". The reverse is also in this case that, "if they cannot stop you, they just have to accept you". When you desire to be great, the world will fight against you by all means, but, when you remain undaunted, they will allow you if you possess the Spirit for greatness. The great contestant or the person who is aspiring to be renowned must have this as a principle never to give up his godly desires. Just stick to your vision and see your mission as possible.

The strong man never quit.

Apostle Paul said in his letter; in *Philippians 3:13-14;"Brethren, I count not myself to be apprehended: but this one thing I do, forgetting those things which are behind, and reaching forth unto those things which are before, I press towards the mark of the prize of the high calling of God in Christ Jesus*

Paul could not beat the Christians and their Christ; hence he had to submit, and desired to be like them after he was apprehended on his way to Damascus.

Acts 9:4,6; says "And he fell to the earth, and heard a voice saying unto him, Saul, Saul, why persecutes thou Me? And he trembling and astonished said, Lord, what wilt thou have me to do? And the Lord said unto him, arise and go into the city, and it shall be told thee what thou must do".

The confidence of the fortune seeker or the great aspirant is that: *The LORD orders the steps of a good man: and He delights in his way. Though he falls, he shall not be utterly cast down: for the LORD upholds him with His hand as in Psalms 37:23-24.*

Much more than ordering your steps, God will not and the world cannot stop you if you are able to meet the standard of God; or if you are bold, strong and courageous.

DO NOT LOOK ASIDE

The strength of a man is his ability to ever move forward. About 1996; one afternoon, as I entered the computer room or a business center where one of my publications ("the strength of a man") was being typed, I met a man (Mr. Oga) in that office. When the brother in charge of the place saw me; immediately, he remembered that a copy of one of my publications, which I gave them to retype into the computer, had got missing mysteriously from there. The book was the *"Beauty of a woman"*. He began to ask Mr. Oga if he had taken the book. This man said yes, and the reason he took it was that he wanted to scrutinize my work. (He did not know that I was the very person present). Then he began to make some uncomfortable statements against my personality. He said he had seen the introduction of "The strength of a man" being fed into the computer. In it, according to him, I was boasting concerning how inspiring the "Beauty of a woman" was. Therefore, when he saw the book in the computer room, without permission, he took it home, unknown to anybody in that place. Like I said earlier, I was right there behind him while the man was talking unworthily about my person. I did not reply him but I just smiled as if I was not the person concerned. He did not know me; hence I had to permit him to speak out of the abundance of his ignorant and envious, foolish heart. I was neither moved nor perturbed by what I heard.

Numerous critics and antagonists often bedevil the pathway to greatness. But the person who wishes to be great must not look sideways or else he falls. *Nehemiah 4:3; says; now Tobias the Ammonite was by him, and he said, "Even that which they build if a fox go up on it he shall even break down their stone wall".* What they hear, or see or feel does not move great men or else they would sink like Peter in the Bible. *Matthew 14:30; says; When Peter saw the wind boisterous, he was afraid; and beginning to sink, he cried, saying, Lord, save me* The world can use anything or person to frustrate human efforts, circumstances and situations.

But when one desires greatness, there is the need for caution, on how and where one speaks and performs. Great men speak and act wisely.

BE DEAD TO SIN

Any man that would be great must have to die first (spiritually). *That is when it comes to committing sin, he cannot. The way of man that leads to failure and bondage say; "use your number six and retaliate"; but the way of life that creates honor and generates freedom is to love and not hate.* One must be able to bear and resist evil arrows or insults, critic, etc. God will have to permit you to die spiritually prior to elevating you. *Verily, verily, I say unto you, except a corn or a wheat fall into the ground and die, it abides alone: but if it dies, it brings forth much fruit; says the book of John 12:24.* You have to humble yourself in the mighty hand of God. God allowed Moses to go through the ordeal of a Shepherd life. From the Palace Nebukadnezer had to crawl for seven years as an animal in the bush. Christ went through the cross. Paul suffered beatings and ship wreckages.

Great men die to live.

The Ability to "bear and forbear" keeps a man alive. The dead have no feelings and do not retaliate when insulted or molested. One of the major things a great man must not do is to get angry and be discouraged. Anger removes respect from great men. Personally, when I observe a little anger in a man that I do honor; then, he becomes dishonorable before me. God does not like a great man getting angry uncontrollably. Hence He said that Moses did not sanctify Him before the children of Israel. To portray how offended God was, He told Moses he would never enter the Promised Land. Your own promised land is the greatness you desire. Greatness attracts honor, great crowns, and commands respects. One does not become great by doing so many things at once. Let your eyes be single. Whatever your occupations, endeavor to do it diligently and righteously too. Discover your gift.

Mean men make themselves servant to the great men, because they go a-begging from them occasionally. God is not happy with mean men because they refuse to rise up and walk or take steps of faith.

Great men operate from the realm of the spirit. For example, when a lecturer says he will not pass you without his lecture handouts, as a student, all you need to do is to go to God and operate by prayer and revelations. You will be able to make him do your will afterwards. God will reveal his mind to you as you pray like Daniel, and see Him as Omniscient. It is possible even as it was in the case of Elisha, against the Syrians. *And when they came down to him, Elisha prayed unto the LORD, and said, "Smite these people; I pray; with blindness". He struck them with blindness according to the word of Elisha; as recorded in 2Kings 6:18.*

BE DETERMINED

The corridor of greatness abounds with numerous cruelty, trials and temptations but great minds do not fall and falter. Or when they fall, they rise up undaunted, to continue.

The mind that desires greatness must be determined, wise and resolute. *But when Samballat the Horonite, and Tobias the servant, the Ammonite, and Geshem the Arabian, heard it, they laughed us to scorn, and despised us, and said, what is this thing that you do? Will you rebel against the king? Then answered I them, and said unto them, the God of Heaven, He will prosper us; therefore we His servants will arise up and build: but ye have no portion, nor right, nor memorial, in Jerusalem; as recorded in the book of Nehemiah 2:19-20.*

BREAK YOUR CAGE

God, who made the entire universe, did not create any man to be bound. *Deuteronomy 28:13; says; "The Lord shall make you the head, and not the tail. You shall be above only; you shall not be beneath; if that you hear the voice of the LORD thy God, which I commanded you this day, to observe and to do them".* Everyone is given the opportunity to be what he wants to be in life. It is just a matter of character, location and time that some are seen to be great and some are not. God has given every one a choice of life or death after the fall of Adam. As a result of one's choice of life, God usually add light and love. *Matthew 6:33; says; seek ye first the Kingdom of God, and His righteousness; and all these things shall be added unto you.* The love of God, which is the word of God, does not wish any one to perish.

The world (devil) and his powers do not want man to be great. They are aware that great men live for God. They therefore, do everything possible to subject the poor through discouragements; frustrations and by despising their works, ways and words. The ignorant man thus remains discouraged and thus remains caged forever.

Break your cage now and begin to come out into greatness! Uproot all doubts from your hearts. You can be great depending on your choice in life; so choose freedom from death. Why should you die? God loves you and He wants you to partake of the good things of life. The bible book of *Isaiah 1:19; says; If you are willing and obedient, you shall eat the Good of the land.*

CHAPTER THREE
STEPPING INTO GREATNESS

And Jabez was more honorable than his brethren: and his mother called his name Jabez, saying, because I bore him in sorrow. And Jabez called on the God of Israel, saying, oh that You would bless me indeed, and enlarge my coast, and that Your hand might be with me, and that you would keep me from evil, that it may not grieve me? And God granted him that which he requested; as recorded in 1Chronicles 4:9-10.

The ultimate step to greatness is through desire. Your desire can propel you to a very high altitude. Solomon desired wisdom and God gave him abundantly.

Therefore Give, thy servant an understanding heart to judge this thy so great a people. And God gave Solomon wisdom and understanding exceeding much, and largeness of heart, even as the sand that is on the seashore. And Solomon's wisdom excelled the wisdom of all the children of the east country, and all the wisdom of Egypt; says; 1King 4:29 &39.

With an intense and strong desire; one becomes undaunted, determined, disciplined and diligent.

Genesis 32:26; says; he said; let me go, for the day breakout. Jacob said, I will not let You go, except You bless me.

Without the burning desire one will be tempted to faint, be careless, and be easily discouraged. *Nehemiah 4:6; says; so we built the wall; and all the wall was joined together unto the half thereof: for the people had a mind to work.*

Without real desire, one cannot really ASK for anything worthwhile from the giver and one cannot be an achiever.

Knowledge Is Very Necessary

As I was teaching in a certain class, wanting to explain the applications and importance of mathematics to life's activities, I made a little digression to describe the prowess of sports professionals.

Using soccer as an example, *I said that a good football player should be calculative and must have a sound knowledge of mathematics to be able to excel in the game.* - (I was teaching mathematics then in a boy's school; – Edo College, Benin city, in 1996)

When I made the statement, one of the boys shouted from within the class: *"Football playing is by destiny or natural talent and one does not require any knowledge to excel in it"*.

I was disturbed and thus felt unhappy with this boy's statement for three reasons: **One;** his utterance was designed to discourage the interest of others in education. *Proverbs 6:19; says; a false witness speaks lies, and he sows discord among brethren*

Two; he was personally not interested in education; he lacked the DESIRE to succeed in life. *Proverbs 1:22c; says; fools hate knowledge.*

Three; he was ignorant of the fact that there are pathways to greatness. If anyone would excel in any field of endeavor, then he must possess the unquenchable thirst for education.

The book of Proverbs 1:5; says a wise man will hear, and will increase learning; and a man of understanding shall attain unto wise counsels.

Without knowledge one cannot be great.

You must have the knowledge of **what you want**, **where to go** and **how to get your desire;** otherwise you will just be gambling blindly through life.

Proverbs 2:10-11; 3:3-4; says; when wisdom enter unto your heart, and knowledge is pleasant unto thy soul; Discretion shall preserve thee, understanding shall keep thee; so shall thou find favor and good understanding in the sight of God and man. -

It was at that moment, in that classroom I got the first title for this book – "Desire Greatness".

Do not be a push over. No matter your deprived background, poor personality and present low educational level you can be great if you so desire, and if you are not easily discouraged. If you could recognize that every step in life; even when you fail; is a step towards greatness; your life will be a transformed one. Greatness, though not by human strength, could be attained by the first step of desire.

Desire is a taste that does not settle for an alternative of sweet wine if it wants water. (Quote: Lawrence Ativie Osifo).

"Desire" is importunately resolute.He does not retreat nor does he surrenders. He is not a quitter.(Quote: Lawrence Ativie Osifo).

CHOOSE LIFE: When you choose life, you have chosen greatness. *Deuteronomy 30:19; says; I call heaven and earth to record this day against you, that I have set before you life and death, blessing and cursing: therefore choose life, that both you and your seed may live.* God made it crystal clear that He is a free moral agent. As a creature of God, you have your desire. And as long as there is life there is always hope. If you choose to live, your desire will produce life. When Cain sinned against God, God did not take his life physically but granted him the chance of life. He lived and produced children thereafter. *Cain said to the LORD, my punishment is greater than I can bear. Behold, you have driven me out today from the face of the earth; and from Your face shall I be hid; and I shall be a fugitive and a vagabond in the earth; and it shall come to pass, that every one that finds me shall slay me. The LORD said unto him: therefore, whosoever slays Cain, vengeance shall be taken on him seven fold. The LORD set a mark upon Cain, lest any finding him should kill him.*

God can set a mark of greatness on whoever desires to be. *Cain went out from the presence of the LORD, and dwelt in the land of Nod, on the east of Eden. Cain knew his wife; she conceived, and bares Enoch. He built a city, and called the name of the city after the name of his son, Enoch as in Genesis 4:13-17.*

In Matthew chapter four, Christ chose not to die ignorantly when He was tempted of the devil. In many ways also you can choose to live and then you would stay alive. For example, you are standing on the roof of a sky scrapper and a voice whispers behind you, "Jump," I believe you would not jump. *Mathew 4:5-6; says; the devil took him up into the holy city, and sets him on a pinnacle of the temple. And said unto him, if you be the son of God, cast yourself down: for it is written, He shall give His angels charge concerning you: and in their hands they shall bear you up, lest at any time you dash your foot against a stone.* Jesus said unto him it is written, again, *you shall not tempt the Lord your God in Matthew 4:7.*

*Par adventure; y*ou are alone in your room and a spirit gives you a knitted rope and says, "Put your head and pull it tight; take your life by hanging". I also believe that you would not hang yourself if you have not chosen to die.

*Par adventure; y*ou are on the road and the enemy whispers to you. "Accident, accident, death", I know surely that you would not choose to die. I know you would say, "I shall not die". If suddenly, a car swerved here and there, and then it crashed! The next report will be, "there was a car crash. -"Six passengers were on board; - few survivors". Doubtlessly the survivors are the ones who chose not to die. We shall always be among the survivors in Jesus name. This is the Word of God concerning us. *A thousand, and ten thousand shall fall by our sides, but we will remain unmovable. Surely He shall deliver you from the snare of the fowler, and from the noisome pestilence. A thousand shall fall at your side, and ten thousand at your right hand; but it shall not come near you; as in Psalms 91:3&7.*

God usually permits a man's choice for him.

No one can stop your desired greatness but yourself. Man is the architect of his own fate. Even though you are to inherit greatness or to be given greatness, you have to be personally interested. The Word of God says in *Matthew 21:22 that all things, whatsoever you shall ask in prayer, believing, you shall receive*

In the case of Paul; the Saul of Tarsus, God saw his zeal and then he selected him. **Ifyou are zealous for greatness, your gift will always find you out.** *Proverbs 18:16; says; a man's gift makes room for him, and brings him before great men.*

BE ZEALOUS

Sometimes, circumstances may send you into the wilderness, or conditions and situations of life may place you in a disadvantaged location or position or environment. Sometimes people may deliberately refuse to patronize you, or associate with you. Eventually, your desire, which is your zeal (faith), will find you to the top. There you will not be despised, oppressed, frustrated, or denied privileges anymore but only to be favored.

Example again is Paul. When he had just met with Christ and was blinded; he had the choice of resigning to fate, saying, *"Well blindness has come why then should I continue"*.

But the Bible records it that Paul fasted for three days. He was zealous to continue with God. Hence God sent a man to him to take him out of darkness. *He was three days without sight, and neither did eat nor drink. And the Lord said unto him (Ananias); Arise, and go into the street which is called straight, and enquire in the house of Judas for one called Saul of Tarsus: for, behold, he is praying; as in Acts 9:9&11.*

When God sees your zeal, which is your desire for greatness, though you may be in the pit like Joseph, He will send his angels to bring you out to limelight. *The LORD said unto him, Go your way: for he is a chosen vessel unto Me, to bear My name before the Gentiles, and Kings and the children of Israel; - Acts 9:15.*

I want to encourage you to have a greatness mindset.

Mean people are always ruled by fear, they always move with the crowd – walking by what they see, without their personal opinions; like the other ten spies out of the twelve Moses sent to check out Jericho. They offended God by their doubtful actions. God lightly esteem doubters and the fearful. And when God is not pleased with anyone, He withdraws His favor.

David was always ready to continue. He went against Goliath. And in all his moves, he consulted God. *2Samuel 5:19; says; David inquired of the LORD, saying, shall I go up to the philistines? Will you deliver them into my hand? And the LORD said unto David, Go up: I will doubtless deliver the philistines into your hand.* He knew the mind of God (a man after God's heart).

As you walk towards the true greatness, the world would fight to frustrate you; but they would never prevail. You must not be disheartened; but be undaunted. The book of *Job 21:4; says; "As for me, is my complaint to man? And if it were so, why should not my spirit be troubled?"*

You must neither look at their faces nor their works. *The Word of God in Jeremiah 1:8; says; "Be not afraid of their faces: for I am with you to deliver you"*

You must not listen to their voices. An Edo – African adage says that: *a child that wants to live should or ought not to listen to the voice of a prophesying bird".*

The circumstances and situations of life fought against David, Elisha, the Christians of old and Paul. The people of the world do make discouraging statements like Samballat made against Nehemiah; in *Nehemiah 4:1-3;* **but be rest assured that God is your refuge.** *In Psalms 62:5 the Bible says "my soul wait silently for God alone, for my expectation is from Him.*

NAME YOUR DESIRES

IS IT FREEDOM?

What greatness do you want? Is it to be out of prison? You deserve it if you begin to desire it. God does not want you to be in bondage. He delivered the children of Israel out of Egypt. You can come out of your spiritual and physical prison if you want to. All you need do is to know the great Almighty God as the great deliverer. *Matthew 11:28; says; Come unto Me, all you that labor and are heavy laden, and I will give you rest.*

IS IT HEALTH?

What greatness do you desire? Is it to be healed, and out of sick bed? You will be out very soon. All you need do is to turn your attention and from the things of the world; unto God and not on your wealth or talents or possessions. Then commit your heart or faith unto the God of creations like Hezekiah did. *2Kings 20:2-3; says; He turned his face to the wall, and prayed to the LORD. Saying, O LORD, remember now how I have walked before You with truth and with a perfect heart, and have done that which is good in Your sight. And Hezekiah wept sore.*

When your ways please God, He is very merciful. He will soon send a message of health to you. *Turn again, and tell Hezekiah the captain of my people. "Thus says the LORD, the God of David your father, I have heard your prayer, I have seen thy tears: behold I will heal you. On the third day you shall go up unto the house of the LORD"; as recorded in 2Kings 20:5.*

IS IT POSSESSIONS THAT YOU DESIRE?

What is your required greatness? You want to build a house, posses a car, or do you want to move into a greener pasture? Believe in God. With Him all things are possible. Let God be your shepherd. And you shall not want or lack any good thing anymore.

PSALMS 23:1-6; says; The LORD is my shepherd, I shall not want. He makes me to lie down in green pastures. He leads me beside still waters. He restores my soul. He guides me in the paths of righteousness for his name's sake. Yea, though I walk through the valley of the shadow of death, I will not fear evil, for you are with me, thy rod and your staff, they comfort me.

You prepare a table before me in the presence of my enemies. Thou have anointed my head with oil. My cup runs over. Surely goodness and loving kindness shall follow me all the days of my life, and I shall dwell in the house of LORD forever.

Even in the presence of your enemy, He will prosper you abundantly. God is aware that your prosperity will enhance His work therefore He could provide for you right in the place where your enemies are, and incapacitate them. *You prepare a table before me in the presence of my enemies: You anoint my head with oil; my cup runs over; in Psalm 23:5.*

IS IT PROMOTION?

What is your required, desired, expected, needed, hoped or believed greatness? *Our God is the great God and a great King above other gods.* If you shall diligently hearken to His voice and do His will, and continually abide in Him; you shall be blessed with good partner; – a willing wife or humble husband; godly children as many as you want. – Promotion, Protection and powers as much as you desire. Name your desired greatness. My God is Omnipotent – He is the God of all flesh and nothing is too hard for him. As He says; *"Abide in me, and I in you. As the branch cannot bear fruit for itself, you cannot except you abide in me", in John 15:4. "Is anything too hard for the LORD? At the time appointed I will return unto you, according to the time of life, and Sarah (you) shall have a son (your desires); in Genesis 18:14.*

GOD GIVES THE CHANCE SO TAKE IT: HE is the Merciful God. He is the only one that gives the chance to man. He makes His sun to shine and His rain to fall on both the wicked and the righteous ones. If men were God, they would have been preventing others from bearing. They would have been selling even the common air we breathe into our nostrils. But our God is not like man. **He grants to man the chance to prosper.** *Isaiah 1:19; If you are willing and obedient, you shall eat the good of the land: Jeremiah 5:19; Therefore thus says the LORD, if you return, then will I bring you again, and you shall stand before me. If you take forth the precious from the vile, you shall be like my mouth: let them return unto you; but return not you unto them. 2Peter 3:9; says; the Lord is not slack concerning His promise, as some men count slackness; but is longsuffering towards us-, not willing that any should perish, but that all should come to repentance*

PLEASE; before proceeding to the next chapter, discipline yourself to go down on your knees. Ask God to put *a strong Desire for success* in your heart. Spend more time maintaining your relationship with God, rather than listening to evil voices.

CHAPTER FOUR
HINDRANCES TO GREATNESS
IGNORANCE

Hosea 4:6a; says; My people are destroyed for lack of knowledge. Because you have rejected knowledge, I also will reject you from being priest (great) for me.

Ignorance is one of the major causes of demotions or retrogressions in life. Many people miss their opportunities because of their lack of foresight. *And God said that for their lack of vision; they do not DESIRE; therefore they would not be promoted into His GREATNESS.* Some people lack the knowledge of what greatness they desire, therefore, they are not able to pursue any goal. Example was Esau who sold his birth-right, for a pot of portage.

In Genesis 25:32-33; Esau said, behold, I am at the point to die: and what profit shall this birthright do to me? And Jacob said, swear to me this day; and he swore unto him: and he sold his birth right unto Jacob.

Some persons do not know the advantages of greatness; hence they under value it, or despise it. Judas sold Jesus the Christ; who represents the great and mighty source of all provisions in life; the savior and Lord of the universe, for only thirty shekels of silver. Demas stopped following Paul the servant of God because he loved the world.

Some people, due to lack of knowledge, are easily discouraged, impatient, lazy, selfish, proud, envious, hateful, greedy, angry, filthy, etc For example a **selfish person** cannot "receive," from God, as the scripture in Luke 6:38, which says, *"give and it shall be given unto you"*; may not work in his life.

He who has no great mindset cannot give; and cannot step into greatness.

Some others are not able to recognize the signs of the time of greatness. They, therefore, **doubt,** like the children of Israel who **feared** the physical giants more than *the God of Moses.*

Ignorance of the time of God's visitation is the most dangerous thing in life. It is the greatest hindrance to success. The five "foolish virgins" were ignorant of the time of the bridegroom's coming hence they slept off. Saul, the first king of Israel, was not aware that God was trying his patience and obedience, so as to establish his kingdom forever. He got impatient and he allowed his heart to be moved by what he heard, and saw. He listened to the voice of the people and he sinned against God.

And Samuel said to Saul, you have done foolishly: You have not kept the commandment of the LORD your God, which He commanded you: for now the LORD would have established your kingdom upon Israel forever; as recorded in 1Samuel 13:13.

Some people ignorantly make their moves forward by their carnal powers, like the case of Moses, who killed an Egyptian. Such move can prolong or hinder or delay a coming greatness.

Some, for lack of knowledge, are afraid to venture. *Without venture no success.* One should therefore, be intensely interested in the knowledge of God's Words; and get richly exposed to good events, places and ideas. This is, possessing a great mindset.

Some people do ignorantly invest in seasonal trades, only to lose and regrettably blame God for their mishap. God want you to be great, but you must be able to recognize His timing.

The bible book of *Ecclesiastes 3:1&6; says; to everything there is a season, and a time to every purpose under the heaven: time to gain, and a time to lose; a time to keep, and a time to cast away.*

Once you miss the time and chance, it may be difficult for you to regain it; but those who know their God are never discouraged. You need to know the signs, so that when your time comes, you would recognize and utilize the opportunity.

THE TIME OF GREATNESS

You must know that, it is always darkest before dawn; therefore, you must expect your breakthrough in your toughest moment. When things become too hard for you, I counsel you to patiently wait on God. He will soon come.

In other words, you should pray more, and resist any attempt to give up at such critical moments. Be aware that the gold must go through fire to become attractive; therefore; you must endure trials. *Except a grain of corn dies it cannot produce,* therefore, you must humble yourself before God.

Remember this also, that the way up is down. *You must not despise the days of little beginning.* Do not be ashamed to do little things, to start with. The ant is a small and almost insignificantly useless, but it is a great teacher of wisdom.

THE SIGNS OF COMING GREATNESS

Attempted – There is usually the anxiety to be up there. The aspirant is often **tempted** to try by physical means: Moses killed an Egyptian. He thought it was by power, hence, he attempted by human strength to be a leader of the Jews.

That was the reason Joseph also spoke his dreams to his brethren. He thought they would immediately understand and see him as the one that would take them into greatness.

Be slow to act except that God has specifically instructed you to move. Wait on God. Be quick to hear from God but slow to speaking your plans to others.

Men can frustrate your great plans if you talk too much. *The crowning is by the creator.*

Humiliated – Joseph was put in a pit, and then sold to Egypt. But Moses was exiled, into the wilderness. In your own case, it may be that people will despise you without a cause. They would deny you your rights. They will wish you were dead or out of their sight or congregation. Stand in the will of God.

Hidden and humbled – Joseph was hidden in the prison and humbled by oppression. Moses was hidden in the desert and humbled by the stress and strains, coupled with the heat and cold of the desert.

This is to make the aspirant learn humility. Sometimes you will lack foods, good clothing, etc.

Fired and burned – The fire of lacks, oppression, commands and controls from leaders can burn very well. You must endure. This helps to bring God's expectations, which is purity of heart on man. *He that rules among men must be just.* You must pass through the fire of God's trials to remove your dross, or evil character. All the filthiness must be burnt off to be a pure and acceptable vessel unto honor.

Taught and exalted. When you have learnt your lessons in the school of God, then He will exalt you. God taught Moses to believe by the rod turned to serpent and his hand turned leprous. Joseph was tested and exalted to be prime minister through manifold temptations.

Elijah told Elisha several times to go back from following him, as they proceeded towards the mount of rapture; but Elisha persisted.

These were trials for Elisha. Until you have learnt your lesson by being determined, obedient, discipline and diligent, you cannot rise to your desired greatness. Just like learning to walk, so are difficult, and staggering steps taken into, or necessary for *greatness*. There are often rising and falling before mastering.

WILDERNESS EXPERIENCE

Luke 1:80; says; the child grew, and waxed strong in spirit and was in the deserts till the day of his showingunto Israel.

Every great one must have at one time or the other, directly or indirectly passed through the wilderness of life. Christ went through by fasting for forty days and forty nights. Moses was forty years at the back of the desert with the father in-law. Joseph went through the pit, prison to be Prime Minister in Egypt. Saul pursued David through the wilderness.

Before the true greatness, there must be humiliation. The aspirant must be **hidden and humbled**. There must be the **burning fire**. The reasons for the burning, is that, God wants to bring out the aspirant as a vessel unto honor. *Like the Gold that must have the reflection of the Gold-smith before it can be acceptable for use, God, the great one of Israel, must see his reflection in you, before you can be exalted.* Your wilderness experience may not be in the real wilderness like the case of Moses, and John the Baptist. It could just be for you to learn the act of forgiveness. It could just be a moment, or a few days, or many years of setback.

As a student it could be that you have to stand against all odds not to cheat in your examinations. Or it could be a mere resistance against joining cult in the campus. It could also be that you have to resist every temptation to bribe the lecturer in any manner. - It maybe a refusal to give your body to a lecturer for just a point of marks as a female student.

As a businessman your wilderness could be resisting a pinch of rice or extra ordinary profit. It could be refusal to sell dangerous drugs, or alcohol.

As an accountant, it could be, your refusal to convert the *thousand numbers to million figures* and *your boss threatening to sack you for not compromising*. When you are sacked for righteousness sake, God will promote you into His greatness. *Blessed are you, when men shall revile you, and persecute you, and shall say all manner of evil* *against you falsely, for my sake. Rejoice, and be exceeding glad: for great is your reward in heaven: for so persecuted them by the prophets who were before you; as in Matthew 5:11-12.*

As a man it could be resisting the temptation to marry more than one wife. Or as a woman, it could be refusing to consult native doctors but resorting to prayers to reverse your temporary barrenness. *Hannah went through her wilderness of barrenness by prayers.*

It could be your resisting the temptations not to attend Bible study or revival activities as a Christian.

It could be a moment of travails in pains and sickness. *Isaiah 66:7-8; says; before she travailed, she brought forth; before her pain came, she was delivered of a man-child. Who had heard such a thing? Who has seen such things? Shall the earth be made to bring forth in one day? Or shall a nation be born at once? For as soon as Zion travailed, she brought forth her children.*

*It is a period you receive an unforgettable lifetime experience.*It was a Red Sea experience for the Israelites who left Egypt. Normally, you will forget the pains thereafter, but you will not and must not forget the experience of joy and abundance that follows. It is the experience that will guide you through life.

The advantage of this experience is that God will always give you a second chance until you have learnt your lesson.The children of Israel did not learn quickly. God had to allow them to go through the wilderness, and be re-baptized through river Jordan again after their first Red Sea crossing experience.

The disadvantage is that you will be a looser or your greatness delayed as long as you remain a slow learner or lukewarm fellow. *Learn to fast and pray. A man only rightly prospers as his soul does prosper; in 3 John 1:2.*

CARELESSNESS

Carelessness can hinder a coming greatness. Be watchful! When you are ignorant of the devices of the devil your greatness will hardly come or it will be delayed.

At the very point of entry, the enemy will always bring temptations. If you yield, you will slip off from the top of the ladder and fall to the bottom again. This means that, you have to start all over from the scratch or below.

It may be selfishness. *James 4:1-3; asks; "Where do wars and fighting come from among you? They come from your lusts that war in your members. You lust, and have not: you kill, and desire to have, and cannot obtained: you fight and war, yet you have not, because you ask not, you ask, and receive not, because you ask amiss, that you may consume it upon your lust.*

It may be a little anger, a little murmuring, a little manifestation of hatred, unforgiving spirit, impatience, a little mixing up with the ungodly, etc.

James 4:4-8 says;you adulterers and adulteresses know you not that the friendship with the world is enmity with God? Whosoever therefore will be a friend of the world is the enemy of God. Do you think that the scripture says in vain, the spirit that dwells in us lusts to envy? But He gives more grace. Wherefore He says, God resists the proud, but He gives more grace unto the humble. ....

Submit yourself therefore to God. *Resist the devil, and he will flee from you.Draw nigh to God and he will draw nigh to you. Cleanse your hands, you sinners; and purify your hearts, you double minded.*

Psalm 1:1; says; "Blessed is the man that walks not in the counsel of the ungodly, nor stands in the way of sinners, nor sits in the seat of the scornful".

IMPATIENCE

Impatience can make you walk against your great desires. *Hence the bible says, in Luke 21:19; that; "In your patience, possess your soul"* Personally, impatience has been my greatest hindrance in life. My writings are from experiences.

God would have by now promoted me beyond measures to a renowned position as a preacher and teacher of the word of God. However, I am still very grateful to my God for now. Even what I am doing now is a great work. God has inspired me to write these truths to you. God would not inspire the drunken man in the gambling hall or in the drinking parlor.

Psalm 91:1; says; he that dwells in the secret place of the most high shall abide under the shadow of the Almighty...

If you want to be inspired of God, then withdraw your heart from the ungodly and distractive activities. Come out of the gambling and the harlot home. Glue yourselves to the Bible and make friends with the children of the KING of kings and LORD of lords. *If you want to be used of God then you must throw off unforgiving spirit.*

A great mindset must practice forgiveness. When you do not forgive your offenders; if you lack the gift of tolerance; then you cannot experience peace in your personal heart. This could lead to sickness, and then death to your spirit, soul and body; or poverty to your home. There is no poorer person than a man devoid of peace and good health.

Unforgiving and angry spirit are offspring of impatience or vice-versa. For example, a man could make an angry and offensive statement at the very point when he is about to be paid by his debtor. This unguided utterance may have resulted from unforgiving spirit and anxiety or impatience. Such troubles could begin from quarrels, to fighting then to court case, which eventually may lead to non-payments of the debts owed.

Be careful! This is the reason you are admonished to be wise, loving, peaceful, and enduring. The greatness you desire may be God's visitation to break the yoke of childlessness from your home. When you are ignorant of the tricks of the devil, a little argument may spark off a fire of quarrels, resulting to disagreements. As long as there is no unity and no love in the marriage, there cannot be true mating. And this will delay or hinder the presence of God; which is the greatness in every home or family. Thus the problem of childlessness will remain or be prolonged.

If you desire greatness, please be diligent and watchful. At the time of God's visitation: to remove the poverty, to break the yoke of failures and setbacks, to remove the stones of oppressions; chains of bondage, to remove the curse of barrenness, to release the desired husband, or wife, shall *He really find faith in you? Luke 18:8; says; I tell you that He will avenge them speedily, nevertheless when the Son of man comes, shall He find faith on the earth?*

Will God meet you praying righteously? It could be that at this time you are already discouraged and then you are double minded. At such point God will not leave His blessings with you. The angels assigned will return the blessings. You are therefore, admonished to be importunate in your prayers. When Daniel persisted in his prayers for twenty-one days, the answer to his request, which was actually sent to him on the very first day, was only released to him on the twenty-third day. If you can but endure and persist, your importunate prayers will deliver your desired greatness in due time.

God will but hasten his word (or promises) to perform it for you.

JEREMIAH 1:2 Then said the LORD unto me, you have well seen: for I will hasten my word to perform it.

NUMBERS 23:19; says; God is not a man, that He should lie; neither the son of man, that He should repent: has He said, and shall He not do it? Or has He spoken, and shall He not make it good?

Unrighteousness hinders greatness. ***Proverbs 14:34; says;
"Righteousness exalts a nation: but sin is a reproach to any
people".***

*Hosea 7:1, 8-9; says; "When I would have healed Israel, then the
iniquity of Ephraim was discovered, and the wickedness of Samaria:
for they committed falsehood: And the thief comes in and the troop
of robbers spoils without. Ephraim, he hath mixed himself among the
people; Ephraim is a cake not turned. Strangers have devoured his
strength, and he knows it not: yea, gray hairs are here and there
upon him, yet he knows not".*

In a home this evil that hinders greatness could be in the wife or the
husband. It could also be in the child.

In an individual; it could be in the heart; in the thoughts. It could be
in the characters or activities.

It usually manifest just at the very point one is about to succeed or
finish up or to begin to celebrate or when rejoicing.

*It in most cases comes with carelessness. In Hosea 8:3; God said;
Israel has cast off the thing that is good: the enemy shall pursue him.*
When you mix up yourself with ungodly people for the sake of
business, you are hindering your greatness.

It may be like the sin of Achan - covetousness

*Joshua 7:1; says; "But the children of Israel committed a trespass in
the accursed thing: For Achan, the son of Carmi, the son of Zabdi,
the son of Zerah, of the tribe of Judah, took of the accursed thing:
and the anger of the LORD was kindled against the children of
Israel".*

It may be like the sin of the children of Israel. In *Number 14:11;
the LORD said unto Moses, how long would this people provoke me?
And, how long will it be that they believe me, for all the signs, which
I have shown among them?*

It could be 'none tithing' unto God. In *Malachi 3:8; God asked;
"Will a man rob God? Yet you have robbed me, but you say, wherein
have we robbed you? In tithes and in offerings.*

It may be like the sin of Ahab:

(Idolatry, and murder of Naboth), or like the sin of Ananians and Saphira (Lying). Such sin could be invisible to the human eyes but well known to the Holy Ghost.

It may be like the sin of Saul; who was the first king in Israel; he committed disobedience and stubbornness. God would have established him but for his disobedience and stubbornness.

1Kings 22:44; **It could be like the sin of Jehoshaphat who made an alliance with the sinner Ahab.**

It could be the sin of doubts or fear and fretting. *And the entire congregation lifted up their voice, and cried; and the people wept that night; in Numbers 14:1.*

It could be your hardened heart.

Deuteronomy 30:15-18; See, I have set before you this day; life and good; and DEALTH and EVIL. In that I commanded you this day to love the LORD your God, to walk in His ways, and to keep his commandments and His statutes and His judgments, that you may live and multiply: and the LORD your God shall bless you in the land whither thou goes to posses it. But if your heart turn away, so that you will not hear, but shall be drawn away, and worship other gods, and serve them; I denounce unto you this day that you shall surely perish. You shall not prolong your days upon the land where you pass over Jordan to go to posses.

The almighty God is great and good; He does not personally take the life from any man. No good father delights in slaying his children, no matter how wicked they are. God does give the chance to his creatures to repent of their wickedness.

God as a father always warn His children several times before abandoning them or those who deny Him as Father; to the devil. Even if a man had to cane, flog, and discipline his child, no good and sane man would put a knife to his child's throat.

But stubborn and wicked children do fall into traps of death on their own accord, because they are ignorant and obstinate.

Just like the physical man does fall into the hand of the law and is condemned to death, either by hanging or by shooting, so the sinful children of God do fall into the traps of the devil and are slain; or possessed for hell, by the devil.

Evil slays the wicked.

The evil one is the Satan or devil who is described as the thief who only comes to steal, to kill and to destroy.

However, some of these ones who are wicked do claim to be ignorant of their actions, and conducts. But ignorance is not an excuse in any court of law. God *says in Hosea 4:6; "My people are destroyed for lack of knowledge: because you have rejected knowledge, I will also reject you, that you shall be no priest to me: seeing you have forgotten the law of your God, I will also forget your children".*

LUST:

If any man falls, he has fallen out of his own desire through lusts. God does not tempt any one. *James 1:12-18; says; "Blessed is the man that endures temptations: for when he is tried he shall receive the crown of life, which the Lord has promised to them that love Him. Let no man say when he is tempted, I am tempted of God: for God cannot be tempted with evil, neither tempts He any man: but every man is tempted, when he is drawn away of his own lust, and enticed. Then when **lust** has conceived, it brings forth sin: and sin, when it is finished, brings forth death. Do not err, my beloved brethren. Every good gift and perfect gift is from above, and cometh down from the father of lights, with who is no variableness, neither shadow of turning. Of His own will begat He us with the word of truth, that we should be a kind of first fruits of His creature".* There is no temptation except that which is common. *What one is used to doing against the will of God is what brings temptations.*

UNBELIEF:

In 2Kgs 7:1-9; Elisha said, Hear you the word of the LORD; thus says the LORD, tomorrow about this time shall a measure of fine flour be sold for a shekel, and two measures of barely for a shekel, in the gate of Samaria. Then a Lord on whose hand the king leaned answered the man of God; He said 'Behold, if the LORD would make windows in heaven, might this thing be?' And Elisha said, Behold, you shall see it with your eyes, but shall not eat thereof. And there were four leprous men at the entering in of the gate: and they said one to another; *"Why sit we here until we die?" If we say, we will enter into the city, then the famine is in the city, and we shall die there: and if we sit still here, we die also. Now therefore come, and let us fall unto the host of the Syrians: if they save us alive, we shall live; and if they kill us, we shall but die.*

And they rose up in the twilight, to go unto the camp of the Syrians; *– there they saw the abundant supplies or they met with their great opportunities.*

Then they said one to another, *we do not well; this day is a day of good tidings, and we hold our peace. If we tarry till the morning light, some mischief will come upon us: now therefore come that we may go and tell the king's household.*

The man in whose hand the king leaned is the king's adviser. He doubted the word of God in 2Kings 7:17. The lepers faithfully made their moves and they succeeded.

Do not remain in your cage or be yoke by what or how you see or feel. If you do not take the risk to believe the impossible you cannot be great.

Risk yourself in God. *Naama did and his leprosy was healed.* Paul hazarded his life, for the gospel. If you are a disciple of Jesus Christ greater works you are expected to do.

THE CROSS -

John 8:59; says they took up stones to cast at him: but Jesus hid himself, and went out of the temple, going through the midst of them, and so passed by without getting hurt. Through much trials and tribulations; the way of the cross is the only way into real greatness.

Except the grain of corn falls down and die, it will abide alone. To become great, one must be sincerely given to God. **The cross is where the will of God crosses your own will. You must allow the will of God to supersede or prevail over your own.** *You will have to be angry at sin, discourage evils and fight back on ignorance. You will have to wait on God and let His will be done.*

Example was Christ at Gethsemane.

Watch and pray that you enter not into temptation: the spirit indeed is willing but the flesh is weak. He went away again the second time, and prayed, saying, O my Father, if this cup may not pass away from me, except I drink it, **your will be done** *(Matthew 26:41-42).*

Do not be in haste: As we are about to conclude this chapter, let us briefly pause here to pray.

On your knees please, ask for the Spirit of grace. Pray that God will open up your eyes to his timing as well as enable you to endure trials when you see the signs.
Life is not a bed of roses; you must travail always on your knees to be able to achieve your great desires and to keep standing after rising.

CHAPTER SIX
THE PATH WAY TO GREATNESS

People say that the path to greatness is *'rough and tough'*; yet many are still struggling to be great. I therefore, say that the pathway into greatness is interesting.

It is always how you personally handle it. You constantly come across huddles, which make you do some spiritual exercises. Sometimes you are tempted to be angry, impatient, troubled, confused, discouraged; etc. All these are designed for your testimonies to become interesting. Occasionally, forces bring certain situations across your path. You may have prayed saying, God I do not want to be angry any more. Then suddenly your debtor short pays you with a note of "no more". As you begin to ask him to explain to him; he does not understand. Then you are offended.

I want to advice you that you should not be discouraged by such happenings. *When you fall, get up, and continue with the race.*

Be encouraged. The Almighty God perfectly understands, and He expects you to continue without discouragement. As you continue He will give you more strength to live greatly.

GATE WAY INTO GREATNESS

At the gate of greatness, downfall is mostly imminent. The one, who is aspiring to be great, must be very careful and watchful. If he slips, then he will fall. The gate into greatness is also the place of greatest trials and temptations. This is not meant to frighten the aspirant but to caution him.

God sent a prophet to go and decree against an altar of idol. He was strictly warned neither to eat nor to rest there; and not to return the same way he went. But he was not watchful and wise. He believed an old false prophet who lied to him; he rested, ate and drank; and he died; or missed his promotion.

THE REAL AND TRUE GREATNESS

Many people have made name and money by evil methods. They are not truly great. *They lack the real inner spirit peace. The approved greatness before God is a Life in Christ; Knowledge of the word and mind of God; Name in the book of life, and treasures in heaven.*

A life outside Christ is in crisis.

Nebuchadnezzar thought he had arrived, but God said, "No! *You must be humbled completely. Daniel 4:28; says; All this came upon the king Nebuchadnezzar.*

Solomon *said he did try "all," but they amounted to, "Vanity upon vanity".* But one thing that is not equal to vanity is *the service given to God.*

Only those who do the work of God and do it in the LORD have stepped in and are truly living in greatness Great men are not people of many names and titles, but persons of good names and righteous works.

What makes a man great is the Spirit of the Holy God that is dwelling in him.

As many as are doers of great things; that is those who teach righteousness; are great men and women.

Perhaps you are already a great one in a sense; you can be greater than you are now. You may be very kind and generous even now, you can do better. God loves improvement. He is the God of creations.

REPENTANCE

Repentance is the access to a new birth. Godly sorrow works this repentance. For example, Cain knew he was cursed, he felt sorrowful but *he did not really cry to God to save his soul.*

Judas did not repent but hanged himself.

King Saul had carnal sorrows because he ran to idol later when he was in crisis. *He did not really repent at first.*

David was always crying to God whatever befell him. *He had a true repentant heart.*

The people of Nineveh believed in God; *then proclaimed a fast, and put on sackcloth, from the greatest of them even to the least of them. And God saw their works that they turned from their evil way; and God repented of the evil that He had said that He would do unto them; and He did it not; in Jonah 3:5 - 10.*

You have been told to desire greatness, to emulate great people, and to fellowship with great men.

You must discipline yourself, and be determined to be great, to love greatness; believe that greatness is good.

All that remains for you to do now to make a u-turn into a Christ-like lifestyle.

Let us conclude with these verses from the bible book of *John 1:36-37. And looking upon Jesus as he walked, he said, "Behold the lamp of God"! And the two disciples heard him speak and they followed Jesus.*

Jesus is an embodiment of greatness. He is greatness personified. - The Son of God. – The Word of God - The LORD of lords.

You may love all that you have read from the pages of this book; that is good, but today you are gladly advice to follow God's Word - Jesus Christ.

All that you have been reading is meant to transform your life and to translate you into an excellent estate.

The word of God came to His own (the world), some did not receive Him (the unbelievers), but as many as received Him, He gave power to become children of God.

I strongly believe that my message so far has really blessed your – soul, spirit and body.

Follow the **Counselsof God**, and you shall be really great, even as much as you desire. *And then you shall also decree a thing and it shall be established unto you; as written in Job 22:28.*

Andrew and the others were disciples of John the Baptist. They loved his message but when they saw the true **Word of God**, - JESUS THE CHRIST; they followed Him. Follow the WORD OF GOD and you shall find the true and lasting GREATNESS; and then you will be able to live free from sorrows, stresses and setbacks.

MAKE RESOLUTIONS TO HAVE A GREAT MIND

This day I step into my greatness; I begin to live prosperously as I am made to be. I do not have to cheat or steal to prosper. I am already in prosperity; *life prospers through me.* I can no more be frustrated or pushed aside. God is my helper, and I shall not be moved anymore by circumstances or situations because I am now in control. I am attractive to good people, places and things. I am not stupid. I know what I am doing.

Therefore; I shall no longer be ruled by anger. I shall no more be anxious for anything. I shall not be a complainer again. The spirit of impatience shall not rule over me any longer. I shall neither covet nor fret again. I shall not live in fear any more. I shall be a giver henceforth. I shall love everyone including those who are against me. All things now work in my favor. *To God be all the Glory; Amen.*

Do you want to be ever healthy, attractive to favors, enjoying peace and prosperity, a winner all the time, a celebrity, beyond destructions, promoted rapidly, beloved, famous, above reproaches and oppressions, in freedom from condemnations, etc.? Begin to live in greatness.

Greatness is the lifestyle, which the maker has ordained for you and every man. *Greatness is an abstract subject. It is sort of a spiritual affair and somehow a complex phenomenon to define.* But in this volume, I wish to attempt to bring out the meaning of*life in greatness*with *nine different things the great person ought to do or be doing,* and some other standard of living that are "worthy", as led by the Holy **Spirit.** His will is that man lives in greatness.

1. A GIVER'S LIFESTYLE

Giving a gift works wonders; it may bring you before important people – Proverbs 18:16. Living in greatness is to live a giver's lifestyle. A giver operates in two ways.

First, he gives himself to the great God. That is, he lives for God. *Matthew 6:33*; says; *He will give you all you need from day to day if you live for Him and make the kingdom of God your primary concern.* He who gives his life to God gains it all.

*Secondly,*he gives to man out of the abundance he gets from giving his life to his maker.

Luke 6:38; says; *if you give, you will receive. Your gift will return to you in full measure, pressed down, shaking together to make room for more, and running over. Whatever measure you use in giving-large or small-it will be used to measure what is given back to you. He who withholds more than necessary tends to decrease.*

Having enough and able to give to others is life in greatness. Those who are living great give out of the abundance they have. Those who do not or cannot give do not have no matter how much one sees around them. A selfish fellow is living a mean life. It is not in the character of greatness to be self-centered.

2. RESPONSIBLE OCCUPATION

Psalm 15:1&2; asks God; who may worship in your sanctuary; LORD? Who may enter your presence on your Holy hill? - Those that live blameless lives and do what is right, speaking the truth from sincere hearts.

The irresponsible person is wicked and mean. Whoever wishes to be dignified is advised to begin to live greatly.

Living a responsible lifestyle is to live in the ruler's palace. Man was originally created by God to rule over his environment. Living in greatness is to live as originally created or to have dominion over all other creatures.

All forces; – physical and spiritual bow to greatness. It is not in the character of greatness to complain, envy, etc. or to engage in fraudulent practices. Greatness is fearless but caring.

3. ENERGETIC ACTIVITIES

Proverbs 12:24; says; Work hard and become a leader; be lazy and become a slave.

When a community is looking for people to honor, they usually pick out men of valor or men who can desperately take great risks to help others or to defend their people.

Living in greatness is to live energetically and enthusiastically.Not slothful or sluggish, but vibrant in actions. Freedom from oppressions and intimidation is life in greatness.

4. ATTRACTIVE ATTITUDE

2Timothy 1:7; says; God has not given us the Spirit of fear but of power, love and sound mind.

Our maker has made us light. We are therefore to live attractively. The person *living in greatness* is attractive in every way; such is favoured and shining like stars. He is not despised, but honorable, respectable, beautiful and well sought after. Being acceptable to good people without reproaches is a life in greatness.

5. TACTFUL APPROACHES

Proverbs 4:7; says; *getting wisdom is the most important thing you can do! In addition, whatever else you do, get good judgment. Proverbs 21:22*; says; t*he wise conquers the city of the strong and levels the fortress in which they trust.*

To be tactful is to be wise, sensible, and sensitive. The wise and prudent person has great mind. What brought out Daniel outstandingly among his equals in Babylon was his wisdom. To be promoted based on excellence and sound judgment is a life in greatness.

6. NATURAL PERSONALITY

In John 15:7; Jesus says; if you stay joined to me and my words remain in you, you may ask any request you like, and it will be granted. The person who is living greatly does not imitate men, but lives naturally as God directs. Greatness is never artificial in conducts. One who is real and worthy of emulation is living in greatness. If you wish to be recognized and not to be looked down on, begin a life in greatness. That is, live naturally your own godly style.

7. ENTERTAINER'S SPIRIT

Give to all who asks you, and from him who wants to borrow from you do not turn away; says; Matthew 5:42. Greatness gives to all that ask from him, and forgives all those who offend him. He is kind to all. One who is hospitable, friendly, and impartial is living in greatness. If you wish to be blessed by God, begin a life in greatness. When Abraham entertained angels, he was given Isaac – Laughter.

8. SINCERE MIND

In John 8:32; Jesus says; you will know the truth and the truth will set you free. Greatness fears no one; therefore he speaks the truth in every way and in all matters.

It is not in the spirit of the renowned personality to be deceitful or cunning. The liar is fearful and thus in bondage. People are dubious because they are fearful and insecure. *Someone, who is genuine, straightforward, and not double standard, is living in greatness.*

9. SATISFIED AND SECURED

Hebrews 13:5&6; Stay away from the love of money; be satisfied with what you have. For God has said, "I will never fail you. I will never forsake you." That is why we can say with confidence, "the Lord is my helper, so I will not be afraid, what can mere mortals do to me?" To live in greatness is living indeed. It is living a domineering life as ordained by the creator.Any contrary lifestyle is just existence or living like an animal or trees. Animals and trees are living things, but their existences are subject to the control of other powers besides their maker's. The lives of the animals and trees are subject to destruction any time, so are people who are not living in greatness.

Worries, anxiety and hypertension are the signs and effects of insecurity. The only cure is to be satisfied. Satisfaction is 'life in greatness'.

AN HONOURABLE LIFESTYLE

Genesis 41:41, 49, 57; says; Pharaoh said to Joseph, "See, I have set you over all the land of Egypt" And Joseph gathered corn as the sand of the sea, very much, until he left numbering; for it was without number. All countries came into Egypt to Joseph for to buy corn; because that the famine was so sore in all lands. Life in Greatness is like an inexhaustible storehouse of grains that will be able to feed many nations for many years.

Greatness is a place of honor. Greatness is an environment where one is no longer despised. Greatness is a recognized occupation of the nobles and princes. Greatness is not a beggarly situation but a giver's domain. It is a condition not in wants but in abundance or a place beyond poverty and above sin and sorrow. *Greatness is a place where one is able to afford all that money can buy and as well have all that money cannot buy. It is a place where one is blessed beyond the curse – a domain of willingness to help and not praying to be helped. It is a realm of exaltation - an attractive estate of inexhaustible supplies where other person's problems are solved.*

Life in Greatness is growth and maturity or an esteemed and elevated level of superiority. It is a situation where one has grown beyond self and is now a helper to the helpless, a giver to the needy and a light that shines in darkness. Greatness is being established and standing firmly with unshakable faith that does not beg for favor but favor following. Greatness does not seek to be known but is well known; well sought after and not hidden.

POWERFUL LIFESTYLE

Genesis 1:28; says; God blessed them and told them, "Multiply and fill the earth and subdue it. Be masters over the fish and birds and all the animals.

Life in Greatness is devoid of complaining, murmuring, regrets, sorrows, fears and worries. Living in greatness is living by faith; or in freedom from fear of offences and destruction. Greatness in man is an exalted position of the nobles. Greatness is a position of authority that demands respects from the minors. It is an abode of the gifted, and the possessors.

Life inGreatness is freedom, powers, progress, prosperity, peace and purity. One is said to be great when he is not a servant to the impotent things of nature. Everyone loves to be great and renowned. Greatness is an instinct in living things, distinctly observed in plants closely cultivated together. Within a short period, these plants grow very tall; every one of them competing for sunlight which is the main source of energy to all living things – each one thus seeking to oust the other. We find out that the reason for aspiration to greatness is to obtain power. Living in greatness is to live powerfully, energetically, or enthusiastically. No one likes to remain powerless and oppressed in life. Whoever that is not living greatly, is devoid of power, progress, and prosperity and of course he or she lacks peace and purity. You cannot be pure or holy if you are not living greatly.

People are living great in many different ways. Some possess money and material things like cars, good houses plus fashions.

Some have education, good qualification and positions. Others are recognized clergymen, especially, those who have the sound word and the power of God. *Kingship, priesthood, wealth, beauty, wisdom and knowledge are also great positions and possessions.*

You may not be classified as one of the above, but you can be or live in greatness if you so desire and as well work diligently towards it.

Everyone has his own gift from God. Some are prominent, others hidden but very essential. *1Corinthians 12:18, 22; says that God has set the members in the body; every one of them; as it has pleased him. Nay, much more those members of the body, which seem to be feebler are necessary*

Your own lifestyle in greatness could be in character; that is you are sincere, responsible, and energetic or hardworking and disciplined. It could be that you are punctual and very regular in attendance to classes as a student or you are dedicated to church services as a Christian. Or it could be that you are very faithful as a church worker (Usher, chorister, guard, Sunday school teacher, prayer warrior, etc). *These functional positions are great privileges recognized greatly by God.* You are living great if you are not subjected to beggarly elements. All animals may be equal but some are more equal than others.

There are many classes of greatness. God recognizes only very few of them, especially the true great positions. Generally, one only receives what he has requested for. Your desire can only be metamorphosed into genuine greatness if it is towards the well being of mankind. *James 4:3; says; You ask and do not receive, because you ask amiss, that you may spend it on your pleasures.* You have to know the will of God for you in order to pray or ask along that line.

NECESSARY PRAYERS

Before you proceed into the next chapter, say these prayers: *Holy Spirit, You are my maker. You have made me fearfully and wonderfully great. It is not in my character to be mean and despised. It is not in my character to be poor and beggarly. I am not a selfish fellow but a giver and a responsible person. I am not a weakling; I am energetic and attractive. I am not foolish, but tactful, and original like Christ. I am not a deceiver, but I live in truth, sincerely and securely. This day, by Your grace, oh Lord, I will continue to live in greatness as You have made me to be. - In Jesus name, amen.*

CHAPTER EIGHT
WHY GREATNESS?

There are several and special reasons why you must desire to and be living in greatness.

SATISFACTION

When you are living great, your heart will no longer be bitter because you will be no more envious; for you do not see any man better than you are anymore. *There will be no more greed in your heart because you now have at your doorstep all that your heart desires. You will no longer be anxious because you have faith in the great God. You will no longer be selfish because you have the Holy Ghost.* You will become creative and no longer destructive because you now know the purpose you are made. *Hence you become attractive being a helper of the needy and a light that shines in darkness.*

ALL SHALL BE ADDED

Matthew 13:12; says; whosoever has to him shall be given, and he shall have more abundance; but whosoever has not, from him shall be taken away even that he has.

When you are out of prison you have freedom. You are therefore; a great man and no one will despise you. When you are healthy, wealth will be added. You will have peace and many friends, hence, a beloved of many people. When the yoke of barrenness is broken off you, and when you have a good wife or husband, your life will no longer be a reproach. Therefore, you will neither be lonely at night nor labor alone by day, and your efforts will be rewarded and your life refreshing. *Nobody loves to be despised or reproached. Everyone loves to be honored and be appreciated.* When you are great, you will have these things; – respect, honor, peace, joy, health and all that money cannot buy added to you.

Life in Greatness is the best way to overcome your enemies without you lifting up any weapon against them. Many people; especially Christians; do ignorantly spend their precious times binding and loosing the devil instead of living in greatness or righteously.

PERILOUS TIME

1Timothy 4:1-2; says; the Spirit speaks expressly, that in the latter times some shall depart from the faith giving heed to seducing spirits, and doctrines of the devils; speaking lies in hypocrisy; having their conscience seared with a hot iron.

The world is changing very fast daily in taste, desires and ideas. Knowledge is improving and population is increasing in millions. *As an individual,* you need to consider these things and allow yourself to be affected also to be transformed and to improve on your own personal standard of living. *If you are not numbered among the great ones in this era you will have to take the mark of the beast or beg for your needs before you can have anything good in life. Whichever way of the above you choose; either begging or compromising, the world will still make you miserable.*

KNOWLEDGE IS INCREASING

In Daniel 12:4; the word of God says; "But you, Daniel, shut up the words, and seal the book until the time of the end; many shall run to and fro, and knowledge shall increase." The days of ignorance are over. We are now in the epoch of knowledge – Jet, supersonic, scientific and computerized internet age. There is no better time to live in greatness. There is no better time to be educated; to get civilized or to have a great mind. Whoever that must live in this age (not just exiting) must desire to be great and must by all righteous means attain unto greatness. In times like this when fork-lifts are computerized, doors are opened and closed by remote controlled buttons; cars could be started or driven by voice; where will you fit into if you remain illiterate? You should not just be contented being an unlettered mechanic or trader. It is impossible for the uneducated to sell a motor or product that he cannot interpret it's manual. You just have to move with the world. Knowledge in any field of your endeavor will bring you into greatness and enhance your joy in life.

Education is the most solid foundation upon which anyone would build the ladder to greatness. With sound education, the student, when he gets into the circular world, is able to diversify business pursuit, like jumping from one trade to another with just a little effort. Also, as a tradesman he will easily understand the attached manual to any equipment. Therefore, knowledge promptly enables one to adjust and as well improve in any field of endeavor.

TO BE APPROVED AS A STUDENT

2Timothy 2:15; says; be diligent to present yourself approved to God, a worker who does not need to be ashamed, rightly dividing the word of truth. To be approved as a student, in this epoch, you must operate in the realm of greatness. The standard of education is changing rapidly and the methods of teaching and lecturing are now different from of old. The quantity of student intake per term, into the institutions of learning, is increasing too. The modality for judgments of a qualified person is no longer solely based on scholarly excellence. If you must be considered really qualified in and out of school these days, you must possess an "extra-curricular gift" added to your academic distinction. Where very few and limited jobs are available, you are required to have "a-self-starter spirit", "a creative ability", and "an undaunted soul" to be able to live successfully. In other words, the few qualified applicants must be extremely brilliant to be considered on merit. When you come out of school without an excellent certificate, coupled with the quality of greatness, you will beg for food throughout your lifetime. Without greatness in your character, you will not be employed, and you will not be able tocreate any job for yourself.

THE CIRCULAR WORKER

Proverbs 22:29; says; do you see a man who excels in his work? He will stand before kings; he will not stand before unknown men.

To be approved as a worker – a worthy businessperson, or a civil or public servant, you must be diligent in your services. Only when you are great, you are approved or promoted to associate with great people. As populations are increasing, more clothes are needed for babies and adults; more vehicles and foods will be required also. As a result of the scientific development in this age, tastes and desires are changing. Nobody loves to use poorly tailored clothes anymore. No one desires inferior and slow moving motors any longer. There is more awareness for good health; people do not want to eat detestable foods again. The implications of the above are: the unqualified textile and fashion designer will lose their jobs as they are relegated and rejected. The incompetent engineers who do not have the desire for greatness or possess great vision would not be patronized. The hoteliers and the foods producers with low standards and poor quality products will not sell. Robbery and gambling will fail as 'advanced skill frauds' are overthrown by internet global technology. Dubious businessmen will lose their jobs. More qualified ones, as better educationists are being graduated yearly, will replace the teachers who would not improve. You are simply advised to desire greatness as a worker and render your services honestly.

AS SOUL WINNERS: *Preach the word! Be ready in season and out of season, convince, rebuke, exhort, with all longsuffering and teaching. For the time will come when they will not endure sound doctrine, but according to their desires, because they have itching ears, they will gather up for themselves teachers; says; 2Timothy 4:2-3.*

Manis made of 'soul', 'spirit', and 'body'. When the physical body dies, the soul continues to live in the spiritual realm. Hence it is very necessary for the soul of man to be redeemed from darkness while on earth; in the physical,so that it could live in light forever after the demise of the body. The soul of man is very precious to God, therefore, His word says: in *Matthew 16:26; "For what profit is to a man if he gains the whole world, and loses his soul? Or what will a man give in exchange for his soul?"* The people who are appointed by the creator to do this work of soul's redemption are expected to be great men and women. *God made His ministers flames of fire.* As it is that we are in the last days, people are no longer interested in mere theological stories as sermons. They need the spiritual salvation for their souls, solutions to their numerous problems caused by scientific inventions, as well as answers to the questions about their destinations in life. Only the great mind, that is inspired and taught by God that would be able to win souls in this generation. You should be in the number. Therefore, begin a lifestyle in greatness.

GREATNESS IS ATTRACTIVE

In John 6:26; Jesus answered them and said, "Most assuredly, I say to you, you seek Me, not because you saw the signs, but because you ate of the loaves and were filled. Indeed, life in greatness is attractive. Great persons are attractive personalities. It is natural and in every spheres of life. For example, a tree that bears no fruits attracts nobody. There were many other trees in Israel, but Christ was only drawn to the fig tree. *In addition, seeing a fig tree afar off having leaves, He came, if perhaps He might find anything thereon; and when He came to it, He found nothing but leaves; for the time of figs was not yet. – Mark 11:13.*

When you are great, you become attractive. When Peter the apostle of Jesus Christ achieved greatness – *received the Holy Ghost*, he became attractive.

Firstly, he won about 3,000 souls in the premier Pentecostal revival in Israel. *Acts 2:41; says; they that gladly received the word were baptized: and the same day there was added unto them about three thousand souls.*

Again, he won about 5,000 converts at the *Beautiful gate* revival in Solomon's temple, when he healed the lame man. *Acts 4:4; Howbeit, many of them, which heard the word, believed: and the number of the men was about five thousand.*

Thereafter, people began to lay their sick ones on the street for the shadow of Peter to cross them and be healed. *You can equally help the needy if you get great, so, begin a life in greatness.*

GREATNESS IS DESIRABLE

In Judges 11:7; Jephtah said unto the elders of Gilead; 'did not you hate me, and expelled me out of my father's house? And why are you come unto me now when you are in distress? Greatness makes you desirable, useful to all, and well sort after. If you are a student, fellow student will begin to come to you with their problems, to be taught. You will become beloved and precious in their sight. They will begin to pray for you to live long and to prosper. When you attain unto greatness, even as a common messenger, your boss will begin to bow to your God. Therefore be born again and begin a Christ-life

GREAT PEOPLE GIVE

I have had the privileges of visiting some great men. My observation is that they are very receptive. They live freely and unsuspectingly accommodating. *"Be free"*, they would say; *"have what you want"*, they would add as they begin to offer their sumptuous entertainment. They practice the biblical principles of *hospitality and giving*. They give; not bribery; to those who are in need. That is why they receive greatly also.

Great minds give great prayers to their communities. In James 5: 17–18; the bible says; Elias was a man subject to like passion as we are, and he prayed earnestly that it might not rain: and it rained not on the earth by the space of tree years and six months and he prayed again, and the heaven gave rain, and the earth brought forth her fruit. The Shunemite woman was great because she gave accommodation to the prophet of God. Her yoke of barrenness was broken by this act of giving.

Enlarge your accommodation from one room to two, from two to three rooms, from bungalow to a flat and to duplex. Begin to accommodate the children of God. And God will be adding greatness to you.

I love great men and I love a life in greatness. This book is my great offer to my generation, and it will outlive me. What about you? I want to advise you to desire and to love greatness too. Great minds do not die (their works live after them). Great men are good ambassadors. They are well favored. They have great virtues. They are not despised. Great men identify with the creator. They are patient, meek and gentle. They love peace. They are humble. They live in great houses. They are greatly desired. They dine with the king. They wear great garments. Go for greatness by every righteous means. It is not meant for one man. It is for all. It is refreshing. Great men do no evil. They are kind and pure in heart. Greatness is the gift of God. Therefore, no one can hide it. Our God is great; He does great things. Hence, He could give His only begotten son for a ransom for us. *Our God is a great God and a great king above other gods (psalm 95:3).* A great man also produces great off springs. We are therefore made great and wonderfully created. We are gods and children of the highest God. *Psalms 82:6; I have said ye are gods; and all of you are children of the most high.* Therefore, no mean fellow will enter into heaven.

PARDONABLE MISTAKES

When you know the Lord, no man will be able to frustrate your efforts. No matter how ugly your products or possession may be; God will always make them all presentable. Godliness is the greatness you should desire. If an error is discovered in the life, works or product of a great man, the unwise or the unlearned, which formed the largest part of human communities usually regard it as a new style (but this is not good any way). In other words, people do not easily find faults with great men. Great men make pardonable errors or mistakes; because they are known for exhibiting superior products.

For example, if a pronounced typographical error is discovered in the book of a man that is well reputed for writing, people easily over look it as pardonable mistakes; and in most cases the blame goes to the editors. But if a little stain is found on a page of a less reputable author, he will be accused of being lazy – a hungry author, who would not spell check his work or who could not employ the services of a good redactor.

Greatness is Godliness. *They that know their God shall do exploits.* They are wise; they are gifted. Their gifts make them to stand before kings and princes:

Proverb 18:16; says; a man's gift makes room for him, and brings him before great men.

GREAT MINDS DO NOT OFFEND

Such offenses like anger, covetousness, and woe mongering; are seldom committed by great men. These are grievous sins before God and men. Any man who is great does not commit these evils. For example: *anger* is a sign of weak character. *Covetousness* is a sign of meanness and *flirtatious* living is a sign of emotional imbalance. These vices are anti-greatness. They are like darkness to light; or parallel lines that never meet. If you were a president of a nation, you would not welcome any of these scandals against you. In fact, you would use every means available to you to fight such accusations, termed: "assassinations of character". If you had not committed such offenses, definitely, you can never be comfortable with your life as long as the accusations last. Let any street man carry five women a day, struggle madly to acquire wealth from every Tom, Dick and Harry, nobody would mind or care. But let any great man do 10% of what the street man had done, then his greatness will diminish by 99% as the defamatory news will begin to fly all over the places against him.

Ecclesiastics 10:1, 5, 6; says; as dead flies cause the ointment of the apothecary to send forth a stinking savor; so does a little folly him that is in reputation for wisdom and honor. There is an evil, which I have seen under the sun, as an error, which proceeds from the ruler: Folly is set in great dignity, and the rich sit in low place. The reasons we do not see great men with evils are that they have reached such an elevated position where no one contends with them anymore. Their jobs are not delayed anymore. No one doubts them anymore, etc. They no longer buy from the common market. Their prices are no longer haggled. They are no longer in such state of wants as *"to eat all* today and then die" or worse still to eat in any shamble where they could be despised. When they are in sorrow, they have music. Their children have toys. They personally have advisers and counselors and well–wishers. They have grown beyond looking at their own problems. When a man has grown beyond his own problems, then he becomes mainly occupied by the problems of others. Such a one who has attained this status is said to be great. When you are living greatly, only then you will know the joy of life. If you are a Christian and you are living in greatness, then you will experience the joy of serving God.

WILL OF GOD FOR YOU

Psalms 91:14; says as he has set his love upon me, therefore; will I deliver him. I will set him on high because he has known my name. Glory is to the creator of the universe for His Omnipotent power, Omniscient knowledge and wisdom and for His Omnipresent Spirit. *The will of God is that the world will see His Glory on His children.* God is wise and He expects man to be aware of His presence even though we do not see Him physically. When any man acknowledges the creator; he begins a life in greatness. *Proverbs 1:7; says; the fear of the Lord is the beginning of knowledge: but fools despise wisdom and instruction.* The knowledge of the God of creation is the power of life. Faith in the omnipresent spirit of the owner of the universe is the greatness attained. God is fully aware that your degree of greatness will greatly enhance His own work. He would, therefore, do everything to make His servants great. However, there are conditions, which He would love them to meet. These conditions are for the good of His servants. For example, it embarrasses God when a priest is found drunk. A public figure should not be a drunk or a drug addict.

GOD DOES NOT USE A NOVICE

A novice is a beginner or someone who lacks experience. The mind of the almighty God is that His servants must be patient, obedient, diligent, discipline, wise, and as well have the ambition to excel. The great man should not easily be discouraged or disheartened, anxious, covetous, carnally minded; and must not be ignorant of the devices of Satan.

1Timothy 3:1-7; says; this is a true saying; if a man desires the office of a bishop he desires a good work. A bishop then must be blameless. - The husband of one wife, vigilant, and sober, of good behavior, given to hospitality, apt to teach; not given to wine, no striker, not greedy of filthy lucre; but patient. Not a brawler, not covetous; one that rules well his own house, having his children in subjection with all gravity. For if a man does not know how to govern his own house; how shall he take care of the church of God? Not a novice, lest being lifted up with pride he fall into the condemnation of the devil. Moreover he must have a good report of them, which are without, lest he fall into reproach and the snare of the enemy.

OCCUPY TILL I COME

The heartbeat of God is for man to occupy till He comes. Therefore, you must be in form or functional as a child of the creator. In *Revelation 3:15, 16, 21; the bible says;* "If you are lukewarm", He says, *"I will spur you out of my mouth". To him that overcomes will I grant to sit with me in my throne, even as I also overcame, and am sit down with my father in His throne.* The man who refused to trade with his talent was sentence to hell. But the man that multiplied his own was loved and added to. *For unto every one that has shall be given, and he shall have abundance: but from him that has not shall be taken away even that which he has. Matthew 25:28-30And cast you the unprofitable servant into the outer darkness: there shall be weeping and gnashing of teeth.* God desires His children to be great - greater than the devil, hence He created man and said, "Have dominion". *Genesis 1:26-28; Let us make man in our image, after our likeness: and let them have dominion over the fishes in the sea, and over the fowls of the air, and over the cattle, and over all the earth, and over every creeping thing that creeps upon the earth. So God created man in His own image, in the image of God created he him; male and female created he them. And God blessed them, and God said unto them, be fruitful, and multiply, and replenish the earth, and subdue it; and have dominion over the fishes of the sea, and over the fowls of the air, and over every living thing that moves upon the earth .* In other place, He says, *"You are gods – children of the most High" - (Psalms 82:6). And they that know their God shall be strong, and do exploits" (Daniel 11:32b).* He said to Joshua in;

Joshua 1:9; "Have not I commanded you? Be strong and of good courage; be not afraid, neither be thou dismayed: for the LORD thy God is with thee wherever you go. He told Gideon and Jeremiah, *"Fear not".* Living in greatness is good. It has advantages. Great men usually have their names immortalized – The Heroes of faith in Hebrews chapter eleven. God loves great men and He encourages them. If your prayer is, "God make me great, "God then will become delighted in you.

ALL GROWS

You will observe that the world is not static. Plants grow; animals grow. Whatever that does not grow is not of nature. Men establish businesses, and they expect growth. People marry and they expect children.

When a marriage is productive, the couples expect their children to grow physically, spiritually, and mentally or psychologically. When a marriage is unproductive the couples are unhappy. When a child of God is not aspiring to be great God is not well pleased. If you are not living greatly, as a minister, nobody will allow you the chance to preach the word of God. No people will believe you when you preach to them. No one will grant you the chance to succeed or to prosper. *Matthew 25:28;* No one will give you the chance to grow. If you are not living greatly, no one will give to you, rather they will remove your little. *Take therefore the talent from him, and give it unto him who has ten talents.* If you are not living great (if you cannot pray) you will suffer and beg for food. If you are not a great man, people will take your good words as mere stories. If you are not great, men will enslave you to do menial labors for them.

Discover what greatness is. The pathway of greatness is very encouraging. They that are living great always stand out distinctly from others in conduct, in product, in their works, ways and walk. He that would be greatest among you must be the servant (Minister of the word of God to men). But mean fellows make men to serve carnal things.

MEAN MEN FIND FAULTS

The Israelites; in their miserly nature; found faults in Zacheous but Jesus Christ; in his great and Godly nature; did not. The Pharisees accused Christ. Satan complained of Job's security. *Then Satan answered the LORD, and said, does job feared God for nothing?*

Have You not made a hedge about him, and about his house, and about all that he has on every side? You have blessed the work of his hand, and his substance is increased in the land; in Job 1:9-10. I believe you would not want to sin against God by being a mean fellow or a fault finder complainer. Mean people gossip. Mean men destroy good works with their tongues.

***Great minds* help God's work.**

Those who help God in His work are usually mightily established like David, and Solomon. Their works are great and ever remembered. The products of mean men are questionable. When a man who is not renowned does a job, I mean a good job, an excellent product; people see it as fake, when great titles are not attached with it. They would begin to doubt and question the authenticity of the job as well as the sources and resources of the producer.

When a friend of mine read "The beauty of a woman" he was blessed mightily but being a familiar friend to me, and he being aware that I used no such title like: Rev. Dr., he began to doubt if I did author the book. When a man is struggling to survive, the world usually accuses him of being covetous. When he buys and delays payment they call him a debtor. When the great man does a contract and he falls into debts they would still believe that he is credit worthy. However it is not in the character of the great man to owe or to be wicked. Only the minors have faults.

Why should you want to remain in poverty? The great mind does not owe, he does not struggle by human power: *Zechariah 4:6; Then he answered and spoke unto me, saying, this is the word of the LORD unto Zerubbabel, saying, not by might, nor by power, but by the spirit, says the LORD of hosts.* The great mind does his work in his closet (by prayers) before it is displayed. But the quacks usually ignorantly make noise about before or as they display their inferior goods or productions.

POVERTY IS A CURSE

Proverbs 22:7; says; the rich rules over the poor; the borrower is a servant to the lender. Even his household despises the poor.

Poverty makes a man useless to his community. *The poor man has not; or does not take good counsels.* Only when he has made greatness that people will begin to come to relate with him. From left and right they will be coming; claiming to be related to him. They will be coming desiring to counsel him and to be counseled. In the actual sense, it is his greatness that is attracting them.

Poverty is a curse. It is not the will of GOD for any one, but the burden of oppression from the devil. Wisdom of the poor is useless in most cases, for he has no resources to exhibit them. No one will ever grant you his or her hearing ears except you are great. *Power rules and receives honors.* The poor cannot dine with the kings, being rejected and prevented by powers. There is competition among the minority for superiority, thus they begin to wear and to tear themselves when struggling to climb at the bottom of the ladder.

Money answers all things. It is a messenger to the great one, but a master to the poor ones. Without it they are unhappy and restless. The rich do not make noise they are attended to. They are gentle and calm. Everyone wants to serve them. They always have additions. They have wider space at the top to operate with little or no disturbance. The poor is usually coerced, convinced and compelled to serve the rich. I reject poverty in Jesus Name! AMEN!

GREATNESS ATTRACTS GREAT CROWNS.

Great minds are attractive. When Jesus Christ fed the multitude with only five loaves and two fishes, what happened? The people wanted to force him to receive an earthly crown. They started looking for him all over the places. *John 6:15, 26; When Jesus therefore perceived that they would come and take him by force, to make Him a king, he departed again into a mountain Himself alone. Jesus answered them and said, verily, verily, I say unto you, you seek me, not because you saw the miracles, but because you did eat from the loaves, and were filled*

Greatness attracts great and honorable crowns. Greatness commands respects. Mean men are detestable. When a father disowns a son, he becomes unrecognized by that very family as an heir and co-inheritor in that home. That child becomes lightly esteemed by that home – a child of non-importance: being now undesirable. In the event of death, the person will receive no burial rites from that family which rejected him. He has died miserably. When a man rebels against his community, he dies like a rebel. No Monuments will be raised or no recognizable burial would be arranged for him. His works and deeds will not be emulated. No remembrance is ever done for a rebel at the end of the year. The wicked, the idolaters, adulterers, rubbers, drunkards are all rebels against the kingdom of God. Their works shall not be remembered unless they repent now and turn from their wicked ways, and plead for the mercies of God. But when a Hero dies, he is immortalized; monuments are raised; and remembrances are made occasionally for him. His works will be emulated. His deeds will be told to yet unborn generations. His place will not be forgotten. *What will you be remembered for?* The bible only records mean men not to be emulated but that the wise one will learn to avoid their mistakes and lifestyle. *2Timothy 3:16; says; all scripture is given by the inspiration of God, and is profitable for doctrine, for reproof for correction, for instruction in righteousness.* Saul was a child of God, chosen to be king in Israel, but when he refused to maintain his estate; the bible records it that God rejected him. *1Samuel 13:13-14; says; Samuel said to Saul, thou have done foolishly: thou hast not kept the commandment of the LORD thy God, which he commanded thee. For now, the LORD has established thy kingdom upon Israel forever. But now thy kingdom shall not continue: the LORD hath sought him a man after his own heart. And the LORD hath commanded him to be captain over his people, because thou have not kept that which the LORD commanded thee.*

CHAPTER NINE
MINOR FELLOWS

I happened to have been present when a matter concerning a young man, his wife and another family was being settled. Their landlord ejected this young man and his wife, because they could not pay their rental. To save his face, he quickly moved into a friend's apartment, but sent his wife to the village. His friend also found him faulty. The matter now came up which led to this young man's open disgrace (as he put it). Then I began to advice him not to be offended and not to be discouraged. I added that he should stand himself up like a man and solve his "problems". But angrily, he replied, "I have no problem"

"Good, you don't have problem", I added; - "Fine; to speak faith'. But show me your faith without works and I will show you a dead faith" My friend, you have problems all over you, when you are a mean fellow. Great men are not despised. *Great men are not pushed about anyhow.* If you attend any function with the best of attire, do you think anyone would despise you? Or if you are able to pay your house rental do you think your landlord would eject you? The answer is a "capital" No.

Minor men are despised.

A man that has not paid dowry on his wife, yet he is living, and mating with her is a mean fellow. A man that cannot cater for his wife and children is a mean fellow. The bible book of *1Timothy 5:8; says; if anyone does not provide for his; and especially for those of his own house, he has denied the faith, and he is worse than an infidel.* A man that drinks to forget his sorrows is a mean fellow. The gambler is a mean fellow. The pastor who still curses and uses abusive language on people is a mean fellow. The so-called great man who will not give unless when his name is announced publicly is a mean fellow. The great man who will not pay his debts is a miser fellow. If you are a debtor who refuses to pay even when you can, your greatness is worth nothing. *So pay your debts promptly. A selfish rich man is a minor fellow.*

MEAM MEN ACT FOOLISHLY

Mean men are full of suspicions. They do not forgive, and they do not give. *1Samuel 25:10, 25; records it thatNabal answered David's servant, "who is David? And who is the son of Jesse? There are many servants these days that break away from their masters".* But *Nabal's wife; said to David; "Let not my Lord, I pray regard this man of Belial, even Nabal; for as his name is, so is he; Nabal is his name, and folly is with him: but I your handmaid saw not the young men that my Lord did sent".* When you are sitting with mean men in their parlor, they feel uncomfortable. When they make their offers they do so with shaking hands and doubtful spirits. *They fear to give for two reasons;* **One**; that the little they have will be exhausted. **Two**; *Ashamed and doubtful*; that the little they offer might be unacceptable.

The minors are impatient, careless and never able to bring out good products. Their works are thus detestable. Except God is in their works, no one ever value their products. If God does not intervene, their cases become disastrous.

One therefore would conclude that the *great mind* or the successful man is a man of God. - Someone who knows God, fears Him, and eschews evil. *Job 1:1; says there was a man in the land of Uz, whose name was Job; and that man was perfect and upright,feared God, and eschewed evil.*

BEGGARS ARE NOT DESIRABLE

If you are watchful, you will notice that there are very few beggars among Christians. You hardly see Christians begging for alms by the road - side. The reason is that God has created all His children in His own image and likeness. His Children are princes and princesses. They despise begging. So if you are a beggar you are not maintaining your name as a child of God. Please get up and begin to give to the work of God instead of sitting down there idle and lazily waiting to be fed from the crumbs that fall from the children's table.

GOD'S PURPOSES FOR GREATNESS

God makes a man great to: -

"Humble him"*And he said unto me, my grace is sufficient for thee: for my strength is made perfect in weakness.2Corinthians 12:9; most gladly will I rather glory in my infirmities that the power of Christ may rest upon me*

To "Glorify Hs name":- *John 15:8; says herein is my father glorified, that you bear much fruit; so shall you be my disciples*

"To subdue the kingdom of the enemy" *See, I have this day set you over the nations and over the kingdoms, to root out, and to pull*

*down, and to destroy, and to throw down, to build, and to plant;
says; Jeremiah 1:10.*

"To prove His greatness and power" *Exodus 9:16; says; in very deed for this cause have I raised you up, for to show you my power; and that my name may be declared throughout all the earth.*

PRAYER: Wait! Do not rush to drop this book. I counsel you to pray first of all on your knees. Ask for the Spirit of determination to continue a life in greatness. *Ask for a Great mind.*